SOLUTIONS
TO YOUR
WRITING PROBLEMS

SOLUTIONS TO YOUR WRITING PROBLEMS

by

Leon Gersten

Director of English
Deer Park, Union Free School District
Long Island, New York

and

Arthur Traiger

Assistant Principal—Supervision, English
Martin Van Buren High School
Queens, New York

Barron's Educational Series, Inc.

Woodbury, New York • London • Toronto

All inquiries should be addressed to:
Barron's Educational Series, Inc.
112 Crossways Park Drive
Woodbury, N.Y. 11797

Library of Congress Catalog Card No. 80-10089
International Standard Book No. 0-8120-0873-1

Library of Congress Cataloging in Publication Data

Gersten, Leon.
  Solutions to your writing problems.

  SUMMARY: Presents the various kinds of writing, the
stages of writing, and special skills for developing
style, structure, and clarity.
  1. English language — Composition and exercises.
[1. English language — Composition and exercises]
I. Traiger, Arthur, joint author.   II. Title.
PE1413.G44   808'.042   80-10089
ISBN 0-8120-0873-1

PRINTED IN THE UNITED STATES OF AMERICA

12345   045   9876543

CONTENTS

Preface vii

ONE **Kinds of Writing**   **1**

How do I write a character sketch? 2
How do I describe what I see? 7
How do I write a formal composition? 12
How do I write an informal essay? 16
How do I tell a story? 21
How do I write a persuade? 28
How do I write a summary? 32
How do I write a resume letter to apply for a job? 36
How do I write a letter of complaint? 42

TWO **Critical Writing**   **47**

How do I write a literature essay answer for a test? 48
How do I analyze a character? 52
How do I analyze a poem? 57
How do I write a book report? 62
How do I write a movie review? 68
How do I write an editorial? 72
How do I write a letter to the editor? 75

THREE **Stages of Writing**   **79**

How do I make an outline? 80
How do I write a composition from an outline? 82
How do I begin a composition? 85
How do I end a composition? 88
How do I decide on a title? 91
How do I develop a piece of writing from a title itself? 94
How do I proofread what I write? 96

FOUR **Special Skills that Develop Style and Clarity**   **101**

How can commas help my writing? 102
How do I enrich my vocabulary in writing? 106
Why is usage so important? 110
How do I avoid cliches? 115
How do I use imagery in my writing? 118
How do I use analogy in my writing? 124
How do I make comparisons? 128
How do I make contrasts? 132
How do I use dialogue in my writing? 136

FIVE   **Techniques that Develop Structure and Clarity**   **141**

How can I improve the structure? 142
How do I decide which point of view to use? 147
How do I write coherently? 152
How do I support a general statement? 156
How do I use specific information in my writing? 161
How do I show cause and effect? 172
How do I build to a climax? 177
How do I achieve unity in my writing? 180

SIX   **Preparing for Writing Competency Tests**   **183**

PREFACE

Communicating your thoughts in writing is a process that follows sequential stages of thinking and that requires constant practice. The purpose of this book is to illustrate those stages of thinking that make writing not only effective, but also fun, and to provide you with opportunities to practice your skill.

The book is easy to use. There are five chapters, each dealing with a particular phase of writing. Each chapter contains several sections that specifically show readers how to utilize their thinking for clear communication. For example, if users of this book are unfamiliar with how a movie review is composed, they will turn to Chapter Two and read the section titled How Do I Write a Movie Review? This section will show them, step by step, the basic elements of a movie review.

Each chapter provides patterns for success that provide a framework around which students can build their essay. These patterns will help them organize their thoughts and structure their paragraphs.

All students can learn to write effectively. The secret lies in careful preparation, logical analysis, and sequential arrangement of ideas. This book develops these skills.

In Chapter One, we have presented several situations. These topics are kinds of writing that can be applied to a variety of situations. For instance, the skills you practice in this chapter may be applied to other writing assignments in later chapters. You may wish to use persuasion while writing a formal composition or use description within the confines of an informal essay. These types of writing are also applicable to the critical skills that are presented in Chapter Two. You may wish to use satire in a movie review. In other words, the basic writing skills developed in Chapter One will enable you to handle other writing situations.

Writing is an art form that has no limits on its subject and focus. There are as many situations to write about as there are human experiences.

ACKNOWLEDGMENTS

Thanks are due to the following copyright owners and their publishers for permission to reprint copyrighted material:

Dodd, Mead & Company, Inc. for "I Meant To Do My Work Today" from THE LONELY DANCER AND OTHER POEMS by Richard Le Gallienne. Copyright 1913 by Dodd, Mead & Company. Copyright renewed 1941 by Richard Le Gallienne. Reprinted by permission.

Doubleday & Company, Inc. for a selection from OF HUMAN BONDAGE by W. Somerset Maugham. Reprinted by permission.

Harcourt Brace Jovanovich, Inc. for a selection from "A Worn Path" by Eudora Welty from A CURTAIN OF GREEN AND OTHER STORIES by Eudora Welty. Reprinted by permission. And, for a selection from CRESS DELAHANTY by Jessamyn West. Reprinted by permission.

Macmillan Publishing Co., Inc. for lines from "Sea Fever" by John Masefield. Reprinted by permission.

The New York Times Company for "Planes in Beirut" © 1976 by The New York Times Company. Reprinted by permission.

Simon & Schuster, Inc. for a selection from "The Mother" by Paddy Chayefsky from TELEVISION PLAYS by Paddy Chayefsky. Reprinted by permission.

Toni Strassman for a selection from "The White Circle" by John Bell Clayton. First published in *Harper's Magazine*. Copyright 1947 by John Bell Clayton. Reprinted by permission of Toni Strassman, agent.

Martin Van Buren High School, *Bee Line* for "Crowded Corner" by Mindy Wolin. Reprinted by permission.

SOLUTIONS
TO YOUR
WRITING PROBLEMS

Chapter One

KINDS OF WRITING

In Chapter One, we have selected several categories. The questions raised parallel a variety of assignments students normally get in English classes. These are assignments you are expected to handle competently, both in style and skill. These questions are included in this chapter to familiarize you better with the extent of the writing challenges you will face. Follow the patterns closely and see that all writing falls into logical, understandable steps.

HOW DO I WRITE A CHARACTER SKETCH?

(Credit: United Press International.)

What sort of man do you think he is?
What is he expressing with his face?
What does he do for a living?

ASSIGNMENT

Your English teacher asks you to write a sketch of a person you know well. You are to describe the qualities that make this person, in your opinion, unusual or outstanding.

How do you go about writing this?

Procedure

STEP 1: THINK BEFORE YOU WRITE

Consider carefully all the people involved in your life — your parents, your brother or sister, your friends, your relatives, perhaps your neighbors — and judge how well you know each one. Try to decide which one you know better than all the others, which one stands out as a unique person, which one has impressed you as a unique individual. Measure your relationship through the years with each.

STEP 2: MAKE A DECISION

Now, after thinking about all these personalities, you are ready to make a decision. Your guideline is: Which *one* person do I know so well, do I admire so much, do I look up to as possessing admirable traits? When you have answered this question, write that person's name down on a piece of paper.

STEP 3: DEFINE THE PERSON

Now that you know whom you want to portray in writing, ask yourself: "What is there about this individual that is *most striking* to me?" Then, under the person's name, list three outstanding qualities that come to mind.

STEP 4: OUTLINE

You are now in the process of outlining your thoughts before setting them down on paper. This preparation is vital because before you can begin to write anything, you must know exactly what it is you wish to convey about this person. Think of this stage as a blueprint an architect draws up first before the house is actually constructed.

Let us say, for example, you have chosen to write a portrait of your father, who is a remarkable human being. The outline may look like this:

My Father, James Allison
1. Considerate
2. Active
3. Talented

This is a good beginning but the three traits should be clarified further to make them more specific. In other words, in what way is Mr. Allison considerate? How active is he, and in which areas? In what respect is he talented?

When this is decided, your more complete outline may look like this:

My Father, James Allison

1. Considerate
    A. He always thinks of his family's needs.
    B. He always inquires about our problems.
2. Active
    A. He keeps healthy by exercising daily.
    B. He is involved in the community.
3. Talented
    A. He is a natural handyman around the house.
    B. He is creative when it comes to art.

STEP 5: TRANSITION

You now have not just an outline but the skeleton of your total paper. All that is required now is that you include examples of the actions you have indicated about your father. The amended outline, complete with information, may look like this:

James Allison, A Unique Father

1. Considerate
    A. He always thinks of his family's needs.
       Example: When my grandmother was ailing, he took her home to live with us.
    B. He always inquires about our problems.
       Example: When I was having difficulty with my subjects, he helped me to pass.
2. Active
    A. He keeps healthy by exercising daily.
       Example: He jogs two miles a day, plays tennis, and cycles.
    B. He is involved in the community.
       Example: He is a member of the school board, a volunteer fireman, and president of the civic action group.
3. Talented
    A. He is a natural handyman around the house.
       Example: He built an extension all by himself.
    B. He is creative when it comes to art.
       Example: His paintings have been exhibited and his macrame work is all over the house.

Putting all this together is now a simple matter. All you need is an original, exciting opening line and you're on your way to completing a sketch of this unusual man.

STEP 6: INTEREST THE READER

What is the very first thing you wish to say about your father? How will you stimulate the reader, in this case the teacher, to want to read on and enjoy this picture of your father? The very first line you set down, then, is crucial. Avoid slang expressions like "My father is a real great guy." Avoid jumping too quickly into the character of your father, as "My father is an active, talented, and considerate man." Some possibilities may be:

Introductory sentence 1: "Everyone has a father to speak of, but I have a father to sing of."

Introductory sentence 2: "The older I get, the more I realize what a rare man my father is."

Introductory sentence 3: "I've seen a lot of good fathers, but mine is by far the best."

Any one of these three opening lines would be sufficient to awaken the reader to the idea you wish to get across: that your father is a special human being. As a result, whatever you go on to describe about this man will be of special value to whomever reads the paper.

STEP 7: PARAGRAPH AND ORGANIZE

The rest is now a matter of taking the ideas set down in the outline and presenting them in a coherent manner. In final form, your paper might look like this:

James Allison, A Unique Father

The older I get, the more I realize what a rare man my father is. As a parent, as a friend, as a human being, he succeeds in making the lives of people he loves fuller and richer. Luckily, I was born his son, for knowing him has made me aware that concern for others, hard work, and social awareness are the ingredients of a happy life.

Father always put his family first before himself. Unselfish about his own needs, he is constantly aware of the pain and suffering of those near and dear to him. In times of illness, of family disputes, of emotional distress, my kindly father involves himself in some helpful, constructive way. For example, when my grandmother was hospitalized, father took off from work to tend to her at her bedside, and then insisted, when she was released, she stay with us until she was fully recovered. He is often helpful with me when I have some difficulty with school, such as a subject like math which I was failing. Thanks to him and his patient explanations, I was able to pass at the end of the term.

I can't imagine any man more active than father, to whom physical and mental fitness are vital. Every day before work, he jogs two miles, in rain or shine. Also, a weekly tennis hour keeps him trim and firm. Our family bicycle is used more by him than by anyone else. His active nature takes him outside of our family to the community where he serves on the school board, volunteers to assist the fire department, and acts as president of the neighborhood civic action group. In this last role, he has brought about many changes that have bettered the area.

Father is more than a man of action; he is by nature very artistic. For example, there is no job around the house he cannot do. Never once, with his skill, has a plumber or an electrician been called to the house. Amazingly, he just knows what to do. Even our extension to the house is the product of his genius. Painting nature scenes comes as easily to him as basketball to me. In the quiet of our basement, father has turned out very beautiful impressive pictures, many of which have been shown in local exhibits. Obviously, he has the innate ability, but he also possesses patience and the willingness to learn. Anyone who visits our home is amazed at the intricate macrame work he has done in his free time.

STEP 8: CONCLUDE

Now you are ready to round out this portrait with some concluding statement that reemphasizes the three major areas you have covered. In the conclusion it is wise to refer to some observation you made in the introduction. Therefore, reread the opening paragraph for some clue as to how you will conclude. The ending may read as follows:

I guess I was just plain lucky to be born the son of this unique man. The more I become aware of him, the more I appreciate his considerate nature, his liveliness and wide activities, and his unquestionable talents. I just hope, when I am a father myself, I will be a credit to my own family in the very same way father has been to his. It is a goal I yearn for.

STEP 9: EVALUATE

If you examine the sketch carefully, you will note you have a unified, tightly organized view of a person who has certain qualities that people will admire. The warm introduction and fitting conclusion balance the description and give it proper form.

Note: The structure of this paper may be used not just for a description of your father, but for any other person worthy of such a tribute.

Follow-Up Exercises

Write a character sketch of:

1. A Hero

2. A person you would like to be

3. A person you dislike

4. An actor or actress whose films you like

5. A politician in the news

6. A famous person in history

7. Your best friend

8. A very ordinary person

HOW DO I DESCRIBE WHAT I SEE?

(Credit: Leo de Wys, Inc.)

What do you see in this scene?
Can you describe what you see in words?

ASSIGNMENT

Write a full description of a scene with which you are familiar. Include three details that characterize this place. Write it in such a way that readers will feel they are actually there.

How do you write this?

Procedure

Description relies heavily on our powers of observation, our ability to record what we see, hear, taste, smell, and touch. These are called our sensory responses, which keep us in touch with reality. Of all our senses, seeing is the one we depend on most. This visual sense of ours is indeed important, but so are the other four. Therefore, we must learn how to use them more effectively. As an example of how a scene can be described using a variety of senses, read this selection from Jessamyn West's *Cress Delahanty*:

> After the quietness of the ranch, where a whole day often passed with no other sounds than her own and her father's and mother's voices, and where the chief diversions, perhaps, were those of digging up a trap-door spider, or freeing a butcher-bird's victim, the sights and sounds of a beach town on a Sunday afternoon were almost too exciting to be borne.
>
> First, there was the strange light touch of the penetrating wind of the sea on her warm inland body. Then there was the constant half-heard beat of the surf, hissing as it ran smoothly up the sand, thundering as it crashed against the rocks of the breakwater. There were all the human smells too of the hundreds of people who filled the boardwalk: ladies in print dresses smelling like passing gardens; swimmers with their scents of suntan oils and skin lotions; there were the smells of the eating places: of mustard and onions, of hamburgers frying; and the sudden sharp smell of stacks of dill pickles, as brisk in the nose as a sudden unintended inhalation of sea water. There was the smell of frying fish from the many fish grottos. And outside these places, in the middle of the boardwalk like miniature, land-licked seas, the glass tanks, where passers-by might admire the grace and color of their dinners before eating them. It was hard to say who did the most looking; fish outward from these sidewalk aquariums, at the strange pale gill-less pedestrians, or pedestrians inward at the finny swimmers.

This is a very effective piece of descriptive writing because West concentrates on the feel, sounds, tastes, and smells of the beach. She organizes her writing around these responses to the sea. Note the sensory impression:

Sense of feeling: "the strange light touch of the penetrating wind of the sea on her warm body."

Sense of sound: the water is heard as "the constant, half-heard beat of the surf, hissing as it ran smoothly up the sand, thundering as it crashed against the rocks of the breakwater."

Sense of smell: "ladies in print dresses smelling like passing gardens; swimmers with their scents of suntan oils and skin lotions."

Sense of sight: "It was hard to say who did the most looking; fish outward from these sidewalk aquariums, at the strange pale gill-less pedestrians, or pedestrians inward at the finny swimmers."

Organizing descriptive material around all of the senses is a natural way in writing because it is a genuine way of responding to an experience. Using only one sense, such as seeing for example, limits the impression you are trying to create. It would be hard to stir the reader if we mentioned only one or two senses. Since it is a total impression we are aiming at, we must become more aware of our total responses to a situation; that is, we must increase our powers of observation with the senses of sight, smell, taste, touch, and sound. Remember: the thoroughness of our descriptive writing depends, then, on the fullness of our sensory reactions. If we understand this, then we are ready to write our own description of a particular place.

STEP 1: FAMILIARITY

Obviously, what you describe should be very familiar to you — a place you know and have been to many times. Ask yourself: "What scene do I know so well that I can easily describe it in words?"

Is it a room in your house? Is it a car you have driven? Is it a building in which you have walked many times? Is it a beach you have walked on barefoot? Is it a stretch of woods you have camped in? Is it an amusement park, a recreation center, a picnic ground? It really doesn't matter which one you choose as long as you are thoroughly familiar with it, so much so that you can convey it to the reader.

STEP 2: MAKE A DECISION

Let us say, for example, it is your bedroom you wish to describe. Ask yourself: "What is especially distinctive about this room?" Then outline your first impressions, as follows:

My Bedroom
1. Spacious and light
2. Sloppy and disorganized
3. Cramped with personal things
4. A musty odor
5. A place for my dog and cat

Now that you have five details that characterize your bedroom, ask yourself: "Which of the five senses does each awaken?" Then add to the outline as follows:

My Bedroom
1. Spacious and light
   seeing: a rectangular space of 20' by 18', sun rays that illuminate walls
2. Sloppy and disorganized
   touch: everywhere you walk you stumble over books, equipment, chairs
3. Cramped with personal things
   A. *smell:* clothing lying about
   B. *touch and hearing:* stereo, television, chemistry set

4. A musty odor
   smell: pipe tobacco, hockey equipment
5. A place for my dog and cat
   A. *hearing:* sounds of the pets
   B. *smell:* the animals

STEP 3: ARRANGE DETAILS

All the items you have listed in your outline are important aspects of your room, but some are more important than others. How you arrange them in your writing helps the reader visualize the room better. So, you must ask yourself: "If someone walks into my room, what is the most important impression he or she will get and which sense will be stimulated first?"

Let us say that a person who enters your room observes, first, how messy it is; second, the powerful odor it has; third, the cat and the dog lying about; fourth, how all your belongings are spread about; and, fifth, how spacious the whole area is. This would be called the *order of observation*.

Since it is important to deal with the most obvious details to begin with, it is wise to rearrange your outline to read:

My Bedroom
1. Sloppy and disorganized
   seeing, etc.
2. A musty odor
   smell, etc.
3. A place for my dog and cat
   A. *hearing,* etc.
   B. *smell,* etc.
4. Cramped with personal belongings
   A. *smell,* etc.
   B. *touch,* etc.
5. Spacious and light
   seeing, etc.

This, then, is the true *order of importance* of details concerning your room. Now that they are arranged properly, you are ready to begin writing.

STEP 4: WRITE WITH PURPOSE

The details you have selected, the way you have arranged them, and how you will express them in your writing have one purpose — to give your reader a clear, realistic view of the room.

STEP 5: USE COLORFUL LANGUAGE

If you merely wrote your description as "My bedroom is sloppy and disorganized, musty and cramped, spacious and light," it would sound like a grocery list and bore the reader. Instead, you must think of original ways of conveying your room's details. Remember that there are millions of bedrooms in this world but yours must sparkle with originality. Try to think of words and phrases that will paint images that a reader can identify with.

If you follow all the suggestions on the selection, arrangement, and expression of details, your actual description may read like this:

> My bedroom is my warehouse as well as my sleeping quarters. Anyone who is brave enough to enter will think he is at a garage sale of discarded junk, but the truth is that what looks like a mess is a perfectly organized clutter of things I value most. My favorite books lie scattered as if struck by a storm, chairs have a way of bumping into you, and the sports equipment I never use anymore is like an obstacle course for a Marine recruit. The smell of my room, I am told, is unbearable. Friends have told me the dozen pipes I keep on the desk smell like rotten eggs, but I never mind. Almost always, Fido, my dog, and Wellington, my cat, are heaped on my bed, growling and meowing like a bad concert, and their odor mixes with the mustiness. Everywhere you walk you can touch items, irresistible ones like my wall-to-wall posters and clay figures that line the shelves. I like to think of my display as a museum of odds and ends, though I admit it isn't the neatest. What is really great, though, is the size of the room, like a tall cathedral which makes you look up instead of around. On the ceiling dance the ever-present rays of the sun which give the room a happy feeling. I'm sure there are more presentable bedrooms in this world, but where else, I ask you, can you see, touch, hear, and smell so much as in mine?

Evaluation

In what *three* precise ways is this a good descriptive passage?

Follow-Up Exercises

Select one of the following scenes and write a short description applying the rules of sensory details you have learned:

1. A day in the country
2. My school cafeteria
3. A doctor's office
4. The basement in my house

5. Looking out of an airplane window
6. Walking through the city
7. Eating dinner with my family

HOW DO I WRITE A FORMAL COMPOSITION?

(Credit: Gary W. Cralle. From Freelance Photographers Guild.)

How can he learn how to repair a car?
Describe the techniques he must know to repair a car well.
Can you write an *exposition* on how to repair a car?

ASSIGNMENT

Write a formal composition giving information on doing something (such as how to repair a car) or explaining a procedure (such as how to surfboard) that would be useful to the reader.

How do you do this? Here is an example of expository writing:

To train a dog you must be both patient and firm. First, you must buy a training collar and get the dog used to it. Second, walk the animal about, extending or pulling on the collar, allowing the dog to get accustomed to its use. Third, make sure to walk your dog at your left side, not in front or behind you. If he fails to respond, jerk the leash firmly, not too hard, but just enough to reinforce the command. The next step should be reward when the dog responds well, with an affectionate pat or a treat. If you follow these steps repeatedly over a period of time, you can train your dog not only to heel at your side but to obey other directions.

Why is this piece of writing considered expository? The writer obviously has only one purpose in mind: to show (expose) how dog owners can train their pets to obey a command. The technique, through a series of four steps, is given. It is information in an orderly, logical way.

Exposition, then, is writing that demonstrates ways of doing things. These things may be procedures, methods, ideas, or operations. Usually a good exposition shows how something works, such as how to plant a vegetable garden. The reader, if he is interested, can learn how to follow suggestions to make something work. Now back to your assignment: to reveal how something works.

Procedure

STEP 1: THINK ABOUT WHAT YOU KNOW WELL

If you are going to explain something, you should be experienced and familiar with the procedures. Ask yourself: "What do I know well enough to reveal to an audience?"

STEP 2: OUTLINE POSSIBILITIES

Make a list of those ideas that come to mind. For example:

Operations I know well
1. How to hunt deer
2. How to organize a ham radio club
3. How to tune up a car
4. What to do when lost in the woods
5. How to improve your grades in school

STEP 3: MAKE A CHOICE

You may know how to do all these things well, but which one in particular are you *best* at? Which one can you explain so clearly that the reader will not only understand but know how to do on his own?

Let us say your choice is item 4, What to do when lost in the woods.

STEP 4: THINK THROUGH THE STEPS TO FOLLOW

On your outline paper, start with the first thing you would do, then the second, and so on. It should look like this:

What to Do When Lost in the Woods

First thing: Stay put and don't wander about.

Second thing: Familiarize yourself with your surroundings.

Third thing: Think of survival techniques, such as gathering food, finding shelter, and looking for protection.

Fourth thing: Leave something obvious to the eye so it can be seen from a distance.

STEP 5: DETERMINE THE ORDER

Is this the order of steps you would follow if you were really lost? If, for example, you believe the second step should actually be the first, or the fourth, or the third, then shift the steps around.

STEP 6: REORGANIZE

First thing: Familiarize yourself with your surroundings.

Second thing: Stay put and don't wander about.

Third thing: Leave something obvious to the eye so it can be seen from the distance.

Fourth thing: Think of survival techniques such as gathering food, finding shelter, and looking for protection.

STEP 7: WRITE IN AN INSTRUCTIVE WAY

When you put these steps together, be aware of the need to be direct and helpful. Use simple but clear language. Remember, your job in this kind of writing is to show how something can be done effectively.

STEP 8: THE FINISHED PRODUCT

What To Do When Lost In The Woods

Knowing what to do when you are lost in the woods may mean the difference between life and death. Too many people get lost but far too few know what to do about it. Here are some suggested ways of surviving in a hostile environment.

Wherever you may be at the moment of losing your way, get to know the territory — the trees, the shrubs, the rock formations — where it leads to, and what signs of people having been there are observable. Familiarize yourself with these surroundings so you feel somewhat comfortable about where you are. Second, resist the temptation to wander off in a panic, for this will only create greater fear. Remaining in one spot will save you energy and allow you to think through your problem better. When you know the terrain well enough and you can think clearly, think of placing something, like a shirt or a sock, high up so that it can be seen from the distance. Others may be looking for you, and if you place something in view, maybe they will sight it and come to your rescue. Last, begin to think of how you will survive if you have to be there a period of time. Search for food, select a concealed place for shelter, arm yourself with a stick or a rock for protection. You never know which wild animals may roam close out of curiosity.

Being alone in the woods is frightening for anyone, but if you follow these basic survival techniques, you will not only feel better, but you may be saved sooner than you think.

Follow-Up Exercises

Write a short expository piece that explains one of the following topics. Make sure you include the series of steps or procedures that expose the way to do it.

1. How to make a piece of furniture?

2. How to learn to ski?

3. What to do in case of fire?

4. How to prepare for an examination?

5. How to travel with a pet?

6. How to repair a car?

HOW DO I WRITE AN INFORMAL ESSAY?

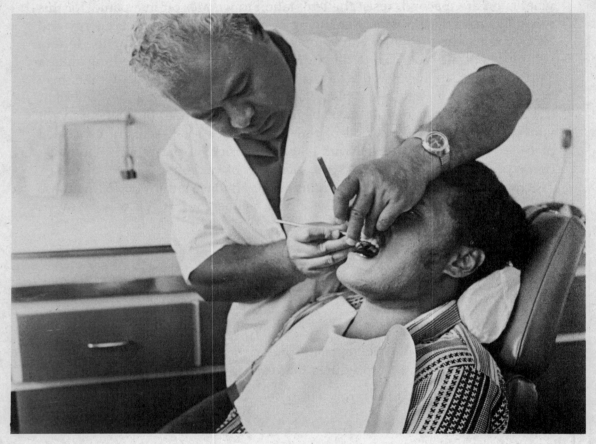

(Credit: Mark Chester. From Leo de Wys, Inc.)

Which man is dressed informally?
How do you determine this?

An essay is a short composition dealing with a single subject, usually from a personal point of view. It is one of the freest forms of writing. Actually, the subject of the informal essay may be anything that interests the writer, who may deal with any aspect of it. The essay may be a statement of personal opinion, a description, a presentation of a problem, or the relating of an incident.

What is meant by *informal*? It is the opposite of *formal*. Therefore, it is looser, freer, less structured. The range of subject matter is wide, from how you saved your money for Christmas presents to how you feel sitting in a dentist's chair. The chief requirement is that you have something you personally wish to say in an interesting manner. What you write may be serious, humorous, or a mixture of both.

Example

Understanding Teenagers

Why is there so much resentment between parents and teenagers? Why do adults feel alienated from their children? Why are kids so ungrateful, so scornful of their parents' values? These are questions that are in the minds of millions of parents across the nation. Unfortunately, there are no easy answers. From my experiences as a young person with stubborn and often unfair parents, I feel that I have some insight.

Many parents are disappointed because their children fail to live up to their secret expectations. Every mother wants her daughter to be gorgeous and popular, especially if she isn't. When a daughter turns out to be neither, the mother feels let down. Dad, who didn't make the high school team and couldn't get into Harvard, carries the secret hope that his son will succeed where he failed. Nothing is ever said, of course, but the nonverbal idea is at work and Junior gets the message. Getting the message is easy, but doing what Dad wants isn't. So Dad is disappointed and Junior feels inadequate and rejected.

There is also a sizable amount of envy involved. Adolescents have more leisure time and more freedom than adults had at their age. Today's society is less restrictive and parents often feel a pinch of jealousy that their own adolescence was not as free. Some adults honestly believe that kids just haven't suffered enough to deserve so much freedom.

Much discontent stems from the parents' refusal to let young people manage affairs their own way — making the necessary mistakes in order to learn. Young people question, defy, resist, insist. They complain, gripe, suffer. They live in extremes — happy one minute, miserable the next. They have great plans and few signs of success. Parents must always keep in mind that trial-and-error is the function of growing up. Parents cannot make their adolescents happy.

What can be done to lessen the gap between the two generations? If I were in a position to convey my thoughts to many parents at the same time, I would offer these pointers:

(1) Don't abdicate your role as parents. In other words, don't be afraid to be yourself. You have your own values and your own life-styles. Stick to them. Being pleasant has its advantages. Even criticism or disagreement can be expressed pleasantly. For example, something like "I happen to like short hair" gets your opinion across without hurting a long-haired adolescent's feelings.

(2) Don't let a certain amount of friction in the family get you down. Disagreement — even though it may be loud — is a form of communication. Friction may be unpleasant, but it's a far better alternative than indifference or silence.

(3) Don't allow your feeling of inadequacy as a parent get you all upset. Read, listen to, and converse with other parents. Don't torture yourself with

past mistakes. Stand up and be responsible now. Do the best you can, day by day.

Gaps are natural between parents and kids nowadays, but they need not be permanent. With understanding, respect, and openness — and a lot of communication — they can be overcome.

Analysis: Why Is This an Informal Essay?

1. It is relatively short.

2. It deals with a single subject.

3. It is of interest to the writer.

4. The writer has a personal point of view.

5. The subject is treated directly.

6. The tone of the piece is serious.

7. The language is simple and clear, but informal.

As you have noted, the essay above deals with people and how they do or do not get along. It is largely a thought essay because it develops the larger idea of relationships between parents and children.

Example

An informal essay may also relate an incident, as in the following:

An Early Wedding

I truly feel that as people grow older, the memories of their childhood experiences and innermost feelings fade away. Of course, this is an unfortunate occurrence, but there is virtually nothing that one can do about it except perhaps to hear the stories of those who do recall glimpses of their youth.

Indeed, I too have forgotten many of my childhood thoughts and ideas. Yet there is one experience that remains distinct and vivid in my mind. Strange as it may seem, I was "married" when I was a skinny four-year-old. Of course it was not a real wedding, but at the time it was very real to me. Recollecting, I cannot believe how maturely yet romantically I thought of the idea of love.

You see, my neighbor and I, both being the same age and the only children in the neighborhood, became friends very quickly. Adults often teased us about being boyfriend and girlfriend; however, I don't think we were really that at all. We truly believed we were in love and would constantly walk together hand in hand. He often carried my toys or coat for me and was my image of a big, strong gentleman. When my mischievous eight-year-old sister and her friend asked if we were to be married, our responses were affirmative. My clever sister immediately took charge and the next day was to be our wedding.

It was a gorgeous sunny summer day and my backyard was decorated with flowers, which were delicately strewn over the patio. I was appropriately clothed in someone's mother's old white slip, which served sublimely as a wedding gown, and an old hat with a scarf draped over my blond curls. Wisteria cuttings were used for my wedding bouquet.

With my sister's friend acting as a minister, we said "I do." Of course the groom then kissed the bride, and the entire wedding party blushed noticeably. I, the bride, a mature four-year-old, rather liked this expression of affection and didn't redden at all. Afterward, I tossed my bouquet into the air. Then the groom, party members, and I feasted on Coca-Cola and cookies.

After this formality, our relationship didn't change because neither one of us had any notion about what marriage really was: it was just something that older people did. However, we eventually did indeed outgrow our "puppy love" and to this day we are still dear friends. Even though he has since moved away, we will never forget that we once shared a dream that all children have but few carry out. I suppose that makes it all the more special.

Analysis: Is This an Informal Essay?

This account of a childhood marriage is an informal essay, for the following reasons:

1. It focuses on one event in the writer's life.

2. The writer has a deep feeling and fond memory of this time.

3. There is a straightforward narrative quality coupled with a humorous tone.

4. The incident is related directly, with specific details to convey an effect.

Example

The information essay may also describe a scene of interest.

Nature's Artwork

Bordering both Arizona and Utah, the Grand Canyon offers a spectacular eyeful for tourists. It is a free gift for everyone, and those who accept it are bound to treasure its visual pleasures.

As I stood on the southern rim of the canyon, I waited for the sun to go down. Peering straight down, I was dizzied by the height but could not pull myself away. The fear of danger was replaced by the impulse to be part of some grand scheme. Then, rather dramatically, the sun began to slip modestly over the canyon rim, and I began to click away with my camera, eager to record all. Like a gigantic bulb, the sun began to dim, leaving the canyon wall in darkness. It happened so fast I barely had time to photograph and just watch.

The next morning, early, I reversed the thrill, by waiting for the sun to rise over the opposite wall. It did, and the entire canyon was lighted with scintillating colors, from the brilliance of fire red to the coolness of sea blue. The whole effect of this scene was cinemascopic — light, images, sounds, movements. It was even more overwhelming than the previous day's discovery.

There are other fascinations to the Grand Canyon, such as riding a burro down the cliffs, camping, hiking, or just plain picnicking, but for me the splendor of this natural mural was the images I recorded on film.

Follow-Up Exercises

Now it's your turn to write your own informal essay, using the principles illustrated in this chapter. Try to create one from the following suggested areas:

1. A quality you have observed about people

2. An idea you hold strongly

3. A funny experience in your life

4. What it's like to be alone

5. A book that changed your life

6. Dreams and what they reveal about people

7. A secret you have kept all your life

HOW DO I TELL A STORY?

(Credit: Leo de Wys, Inc.)

Describe the action of this scene above.
What story is it conveying?

ASSIGNMENT

Think of some incident in your life and write it as it happened.

How do you do this?

Procedure

STEP 1: THINK OF POSSIBILITIES

Here you must first make a choice. Obviously, many experiences have come your way — some exciting, some sad, some scary. You must make a decision as to which one is the best choice as a story, and that choice depends on two things: how well you remember it, and how interesting it would be to read.

Narration is telling a story that has a chain of events. The story must have happened, have a beginning, lead from one event to another, have a focus, and come to an end.

With this definition in mind, you must think back to your past and ask yourself: "What happened to me in my life that I can recall well enough to write about?" Give yourself time to allow your thoughts to flow.

STEP 2: OUTLINE YOUR POSSIBILITIES

Let us say, for example, you remember three distinct happenings in your life. One is an accident you had while on a camping trip, another is how you helped to save a person from a blazing building, and a third is about a time you got lost in a big city. The best way to make a wise choice is to list all three on a piece of paper, as follows:

Incidents in My Life

1. A camping trip accident
2. Saving a person in a fire
3. Getting lost in a big city

Since a good narrative should identify the situation with necessary background information, relate the main events of the story, and conclude with a satisfying ending, you should ask yourself: "Which one of my three possible happenings could I write about in such a unified way that the reader will not only be interested but actually *see* what happened?" The answer involves clear memory, a good sense of detail, and a completeness of effect.

Let us say, for example, that item 2, "Saving a person in a fire," is the best choice according to the definition of narration. Then take another piece of paper and head it "Saving a Person in a Fire." Think of three distinct details that will help the reader to visualize the scene. They might be something like this:

1. A man screamed "Fire!" out of a smoking window while the fire engines clanged in the street below.
2. I left the watching crowd to race through the blazing fire.
3. I remember leading a gasping hulk of a man out of a crumbling room.

STEP 3: WRITE AN OUTLINE

Now place the units properly in outline form, with subheadings:

Saving a Person in a Fire

Detail 1.   A man screamed ''Fire!'' out of a smoking window while the fire engines clanged in the street below.
    a. I stood immobilized and frightened.
    b. I was unsure what to do.
Detail 2.   I left the watching crowd to race through the blazing fire.
    a. A fire captain tried to stop me.
    b. I pushed through the throng and jumped over the hoses.
Detail 3.   I remember leading a gasping hulk of a man out of a crumbling building.
    a. The flames scorched me.
    b. I could hardly breathe but I ignored the danger.

STEP 4: ORGANIZE THE NARRATION

You now have the essential skeleton of what happened that day. Since the outline shows the events in the order in which they happened, there is no need to rearrange them. Now it's a matter of extending the details somewhat to enable the readers to feel they are witnesses to the event of your rescuing a person in a burning building.

STEP 5: INTRODUCE THE EVENT

Before you can actually get into your experience, it is wise to begin in a way that makes the reader want to read on and find out what happened. Therefore, your first few sentences should be striking and appealing, and should lead right into the heart of the rescue operation.

> Rarely in our lives do we have an opportunity to be of service to others. Often, we take life for granted, pass it by, or just ignore it. But then, suddenly, without warning, we are forced to make a decision to help another human being. This rare moment occurred to me three years ago, and I shall never forget it.

STEP 6: THE BODY OF THE NARRATION

With this opener to excite and interest, you can proceed with your three main details. Each one should be developed fully and paragraphed separately.

> I was returning from school one afternoon when I noticed a crowd gathering in front of a building. Smoke was puffing out on all sides and fire engines were clanging noisily up and down the street. To keep the people from getting too close to the danger, a policeman kept them on the other side of the street. I stood with the onlookers, at first curious, then amazed, finally shocked. Then, suddenly, a man appeared at a window, shouting ''Fire!'' A gasp rang through the crowd.

Not aware of what my body was doing, I found myself pushing through the crowd and racing across the street. The policeman tried to grab me but I ducked under him and jumped over the thick hoses snaking the ground. The fire captain directing the men up and down the ladder screamed after me as I plunged through the doorway and up the stairs. Distant cries, smoke so billowy I couldn't see, and flames so hot I could feel my skin scorch made me wince with fear. But it was too late; I had to do something for that poor man upstairs.

After what seemed like an eternity, I heard him whimper to the left of me on the second floor. By this time, he was already on the floor, sobbing, pleading, a helpless hulk. Coughing and spitting, I lifted him and bent him over my shoulder. The flames shooting into the room made me aware I had to get him out or we would be engulfed and asphyxiated. He was like a limp child as I carried him down the stairs and into the street. The rush of cold air on my face revived me somewhat, though I fell to the ground with the weight of the man on my back. All I remember is a blur of eyes, as hands reached out, and a mumble of voices from all around.

When I awoke I was lying in a strange bed, covered by a sheet, my mother seated by my side. The sharp smells of the place made me realize I was in a hospital, but how I got there was not clear. No sooner did I open my eyes than my mother, tears falling, whispered, "I'm so proud of you."

STEP 7: END THE NARRATION

As in all kinds of writing, a narration should have an ending that is as interesting as the introduction. Go back to the beginning and see how you began and then make your conclusion relate to it in some way. For example, in this account of a boy and how he rescued a fire victim, the writer makes the point that we take life for granted and do not consider its importance until an emergency arises. It is that emergency that makes some of us come to the aid of others. The ending, then, should reemphasize that opening point.

STEP 8: CONCLUDE

As I recall that day of the fire and how I blindly raced into a flaming building, I still do not know why I endangered my life. All I know is a man was pleading for help and I responded. After all, what else would any decent, caring human being do in a terrible situation like that?

STEP 9: TITLE THE NARRATION

What you place on top of a narration as your title is very important. People have a way of looking at titles and judging what follows as either interesting or boring. In this case, the title "An Important Event in My Life" does not stir any desire for the reader to go on. Besides, the word "important" doesn't say anything special about that experience.

Which of the following three would fit the narration best?

1. How I Saved a Man in a Fire
2. The Day I Cared Enough To Act
3. A Memory I Shall Never Forget

If you selected the second one, you were wise. It is a title that appeals, that makes the reader wonder in what way you cared, and what action you took. With a title like that, most likely the reader will want to know more about your special experiences.

STEP 10: EVALUATE

Now put the entire narration together to see how the parts fit together, whether the details are chronologically organized, and whether the entire event has unity.

The Day I Cared Enough To Act

Rarely in our lives do we have an opportunity to be of service to others. Often, we take life for granted, pass it by, or just ignore it. But then, suddenly, without warning, we are forced to make a decision to help another human being. This rare moment occurred to me three years ago, and I shall never forget it.

I was returning from school one afternoon when I noticed a crowd gathering in front of a building. Smoke was puffing out on all sides and fire engines were clanging noisily up and down the street. To keep the people from getting too close to the danger, a policeman kept them on the other side of the street. I stood with the onlookers, at first curious, then amazed, finally shocked. Then, suddenly, a man appeared at a window, shouting "Fire!" A gasp rang through the crowd.

Not aware of what my body was doing, I found myself pushing through the crowd and racing across the street. The policeman tried to grab me, but I ducked under him and jumped over the thick hoses snaking the ground. The fire captain directing the men up and down the ladder screamed after me as I plunged through the doorway and up the stairs. Distant cries, smoke so billowy I couldn't see, and flames so hot I could feel my skin scorch made me wince with fear. But it was too late; I had to do something for that poor man upstairs.

After what seemed like an eternity, I heard him whimper to the left of me on the second floor. By this time, he was already on the floor, sobbing, pleading, helpless in his pain. Coughing and spitting, I lifted him and bent him over my shoulder. The flames in the room made me aware I had to get him out before we would be engulfed and asphyxiated. He was like a limp child as I carried him down the stairs and into the street. The rush of cold air revived me somewhat, though I fell to the ground with the weight of the man on my back. All I remember is a blur of eyes, as hands reached out, and a mumble of voices from all around.

When I awoke I was lying in a strange bed, covered by a sheet, my mother seated by my side. The sharp smells of the place made me realize I was in a hospital but how I got there was not clear. No sooner did I open my eyes than my mother, tears falling, whispered, "I'm so proud of you."

As I recall that day of the fire and how I blindly raced into a flaming building, I still do not know why I endangered my life. All I know is a man was pleading for help and I responded. After all, what else would any decent, caring human being do in a terrible situation like that?

Analysis

Ask yourself these questions:

1. Does it deal with one specific event?

2. Does it capture the event well?

3. Are there details to make it realistic and powerful?

4. Is it well organized?

5. Is it the kind of narration that would capture a reader's interest?

Example

Not all narrations follow the same pattern or focus on the same experience. Here is another example of a student who faced a situation that will affect the rest of her life:

The Boatride I'll Never Forget

It was the most beautiful day the summer had given us yet. We had taken the boat out much farther than usual. We weren't exactly sure where we were but we knew the general direction in which to go home. We were cruising at a comfortable speed when my father decided to stop. He saw a beach about one hundred feet to the left. It was so peaceful looking and there was no one on it. When you get so close to shore the water isn't deep enough to take the boat into, so he stopped and said that my brother and his friend could jump out and swim to the beach if they wanted to. The water was clean and they were both experienced swimmers.

Two of my brothers were with us that day. Mitchell, who had brought his friend, was 18. Robert, my other brother, was 22. Mitchell and his friend dove into the clear blue water. They swam so gracefully toward the beautiful sand. They had only been swimming for a couple of minutes when all of a sudden Mitchell started yelling for help. We all thought he was kidding at first and we started to laugh. Then we realized that he most certainly was very serious. He had gotten a cramp in his leg and couldn't swim or even tread water. His friend couldn't hold him up. The water was very deep.

My father didn't know what to do. He can't swim, and he didn't want to bring the boat over to get them for fear of running over them. Robert, who had been resting in the front of the boat, heard the commotion, realized what was happening. He threw down what was in his pockets, took off his shoes, and gallantly dove into the deep blue water to save his brother. After a long struggle, he brought Mitchell up into the boat.

He had fallen into shock. Robert got the first aid kit which told him how to give mouth to mouth resuscitation. I stood watching in total fright and confusion. Never had I seen such a sight. His eyes were open but he couldn't see. He was breathing, he was alive, but he couldn't hear us.

Meanwhile, my father was calling the coast guard on the radio. They told us where to bring Mitchell. When we arrived, there was a helicopter with a loudspeaker telling us that the ambulance would be there shortly. It arrived within a minute and took Mitchell to Glen Cove Hospital.

It took Mitchell about a week to recover. He had swallowed so much water that it had injured him internally. Robert was the hero of the day. He went to Carvel and got himself a cake that said "I am a hero." That was very modest of him. But we were, thank God, together again — all together.

Analysis

If you read both student writings you will note that a well-written narrative:

1. focuses on a real-life situation

2. uses only those details that highlight the point you wish to make

3. conveys the feelings of the person affected by the incident

4. makes a point and doesn't just tell the story

Follow-Up Exercises

See how well you can relate a story by developing one of the following suggested topics:

1. A day I helped to entertain guests

2. A memorable trip I recently took

3. An experience that taught me a lesson

4. The day my friend came through in a pinch

5. A painful moment in my life

HOW DO I WRITE TO PERSUADE?

(Credit: Wide World Photos.)

What is shown in this picture?
What are your thoughts about nuclear energy?
Can you write a persuasive paper about your opinion of nuclear energy?

ASSIGNMENT

In about 200 words, write a persuasive paper that makes the reader aware of a strong position you have on a popular issue. Include three convincing reasons why you hold this view.

How do you write persuasively?

STEP 1: THINK OF AN ISSUE

If you are to persuade someone of your own feelings about an issue, it must be one you have strong views on. Think of all the big issues of the day, those that people argue about all the time. Dash off a list as they come to mind, like this:

1. Abortion
2. Capital punishment
3. Mercy killing
4. Increased federal aid
5. Higher taxes
6. Foreign aid to underdeveloped countries
7. Legalizing marijuana
8. Operating stores on Sunday
9. The space program
10. A smoking room for students

STEP 2: MAKE A DECISION

Which one you select depends on how much you know about the issue. For example, if you were to write about abortion and whether or not you support it, you would have to know a lot of facts and statistics. To get this you would have to do a lot of reading on surveys, laws, and studies, and take a lot of notes. On the other hand, should you want to argue for the existence of a smoking lounge for students, you would not need so many facts, but would rely more on surveys that indicate how students, as well as teachers and administrators, regard the idea.

It is best to check off the three that you know most about and are interested in before the final decision. Study the selected three and ask yourself: "Which one do I know most about? Which one turns me on strongly enough to write about it?" Let us suppose you like the smoking lounge question best. What do you do next?

STEP 3: OUTLINE YOUR POSITION

Just saying that having a room where students can congregate to smoke is a basic right is not much of an argument. It certainly doesn't persuade anyone. What you must do is come up with at least three solid, substantiated reasons to support the existence of such a facility. The way to do this is to (1) survey other students as to their reasons, (2) read articles or news items in school newspapers or publications that deal with the subject, and (3) make your own observations. If you do this carefully, you may come up with something like this, as an outline:

The Time Has Come for a Smoking Lounge

A. *Argument One:* A vast number of cigarette-smoking students feel their rights are denied.
   Support: Survey of school population
B. *Argument Two:* Schools are crowded and impersonal and students feel left out.
   Support: Editorial in the *Flying Eagle,* school newspaper

C. *Argument Three:* Having such a room will help to solve the problem of cutting classes.

   Support: My own observations of friends and interview with the dean

   Once you have this sort of outline you are ready to write.

STEP 4: EXPRESS YOURSELF PERSUASIVELY

The words you use must be carefully chosen. Language should be simple, sentences short and direct, and the ideas crystal clear. Otherwise you may not convince your readers.

STEP 5: USE AN ORIGINAL APPROACH

Since this is not a new topic, but has been argued again and again, try to come up with an original angle, one never used before. This is important because the reader doesn't want to hear the same tiresome arguments rehashed. Ask yourself: "How can I write it in such a way that the reader will not only listen but perhaps be convinced?" Warning: Never begin "I am now going to tell you my reasons for a smoking lounge."

STEP 6: WRITE IT OUT AND STICK TO THE POINT

Remember that you are arguing in favor of the rights of students to a room where they can smoke freely, not about student discontent with the school as a whole. Don't use this as an opportunity to criticize the principal or the teachers or to point out the weaknesses of the learning program. Stick to your focus of the lounge only so that the reader clearly sees the issue.

   If you clearly understand your purpose and the guidelines of this type of writing exercise, you can, if you try, come up with a convincing piece like this:

The Time Has Come for a Smoking Lounge

   While it is true a vast number of Americans are now being denied their basic human rights, it is also true that high school students are being denied theirs. In my school, as well as in many schools throughout the city, the concept of a smoking lounge is long past due.

   The latest study of the increase in cigarette smoking conducted by the Food and Drug Administration indicates that more and more adolescents are taking to the habit of smoking. Among my friends alone, seven out of ten want a smoke during the school day. The denial of this desire makes them nervous and, therefore, unrelaxed in class. Poor grades in subjects are often a result of this denial. A survey I conducted in my senior class involving 52 seventeen- and eighteen-year-olds shows a high degree of need for a place where they can relax with a cigarette. One senior boy, when I questioned him, said, "For six hours a day I cannot light up because of school restrictions. I feel my rights have been denied."

   Young people in a big urban high school are shuffled about like cattle and they have little time for socialization with their friends. A smoking lounge, where they can go during their free period, would allow them the chance to make personal contact as well as to smoke. Smoking and talking are clearly linked as social patterns of behavior. In a recent editorial in our school newspaper, *Flying Eagle*, a student writes: "As one of many in a huge school, I feel left out and unrecognized. This makes me turn to a cigarette for comfort. But how can I in the building?"

There are many reasons why students cut, but an important one is that their need to smoke is so great that they will risk the penalty of cutting. In my case, for example, I have not gone to several subject classes because my craving could not be controlled. And while outside, the temptation to remain was even greater. A smoking lounge in our school would undoubtedly cut down on those tempted to break out. Recently, I visited the dean and asked him, "Are you in favor of a smoking lounge?" He answered very honestly, "It sure would make my job a lot easier. Besides, it would make the school a cleaner place, not having to be bothered with sweeping up cigarette butts all over the building."

There are, of course, many other reasons I can use for the creation of a smoking area for smokers in our school, but for the three important reasons I have stated — the rights of cigarette smokers to their habit, the need to socialize and relax, and as a partial solution to cutting — the school administration should recognize that the longer they resist, the longer will the need be. In the year 1979 it seems like such a small request in the light of so many bigger issues. So why dwell on it any longer? Let's get on with finding the room that will welcome students with cigarettes in their hands.

STEP 7: EVALUATE YOUR WRITING

You must always reread any piece of writing before you hand it in to see whether or not it accomplishes its purpose. In the piece above, does the writer convince you of the need for a smoking lounge in his school? If so, how does he succeed in persuading you?

Follow-Up Exercises

Select one of the following areas of debate and write a persuasive paper that gives three important reasons why you are for or against the issue.

1. All schools should be integrated.

2. The drug laws should be made tougher.

3. The draft should be brought back.

4. Everyone should have the right to die.

5. The space program should be dropped.

HOW DO I WRITE A SUMMARY?

(Credit: Peter L. Gould. From Freelance Photographers Guild.)

Can you write a summary of this scene?

Very often we read a long passage and have to summarize the main ideas, to condense the facts. It involves taking a complicated piece of writing and simplifying it.

Think of writing a summary as peeling the skin from an apple and getting down to the core. If you eliminate all the outer layers of writing, you can get down to the inner essentials of the piece.

ASSIGNMENT

Write a summary of the following passage.

Phonetics is a science of speech sounds. A knowledge of phonetics is essential for guiding the oral language development of children. It is also basic information for teachers who attempt to guide children in the effective use of phonetic analysis techniques for word recognition purposes. For these and other reasons, all teachers are encouraged to include the systematic study of phonetics in their professional preparation.

A knowledge of phonetics by the teacher can help clarify the confusion caused by the inadequate English alphabet. This alphabet consists of twenty-six letters with letter names which must represent more than forty sounds in spoken English. The result is chaotic — one letter represents more than one sound; one sound is represented by more than one letter; two or more letters represent a single sound.

The mere knowledge of phonetic symbols does not insure the ability to use the sounds represented by the symbols in improving speech patterns. A successful application of sounds learned through the phonetic approach depends upon training, which involves: hearing the sound; imitating the sound; analyzing the production of the sound; producing the sound voluntarily; and recognizing the phonetic symbol. The symbols, known to the teacher, may be used discriminatingly when needed, as an additional visual aid. There is no need to teach the students the entire phonetic alphabet.

Procedure

STEP 1: MAKE AN OUTLINE OF THE BASIC FACTS

1. The importance of phonetics to teachers and children
2. How a knowledge of phonetics can help to clarify language
3. How training helps us use phonetic symbols in improving speech patterns

STEP 2: CHECK THE LIST OF FACTS

You will note all three statements are taken from the three paragraphs as they are developed. For example:

Paragraph 1: The importance of phonetics to teachers and children

Paragraph 2: How a knowledge of phonetics can help to clarify language

Paragraph 3: How training helps us use phonetic symbols in improving speech patterns

STEP 3: CUT THE PASSAGE

Here the trick is to develop each of the three statements briefly but accurately. Condense the paragraphs but do not repeat them.

> The importance of phonetics, the science of speech sounds, is that it helps teachers guide children in word recognition by using sound techniques for analysis. A knowledge of phonetics helps to clarify language by eliminating the confusion of twenty-six letters representing more than forty sounds in spoken English.
>
> Effective training in the use of symbols to improve speech patterns involves hearing, imitating, analyzing, producing, and recognizing various sounds as well as using the alphabet as a visual aid.

Analysis

What we have done in this summary, if you compare it to the original passage, is to simplify, or strip down the language so that what we end up with is a bare, skeletal structure. But even though it is shorter, it contains the very same ideas.

In school, as well as at other times, there are a variety of situations where this technique may be helpful:

1. Interviews with people

2. News broadcasts

3. Scientific experiments

4. Famous people's experiments

5. Acts and scenes of plays and novels

6. Chapters about historical events

7. Debates on issues

8. Instructions on how to do things and use items

Follow-Up Exercise

Write a summary of the following passage:

> Ice-skating is a lot of fun but you had better know as much about clothes and proper fit. Buying the right kind of skates and being certain you have the proper size are as important as the condition of the ice in the arena where you skate. Be certain your toes have ample room, that your heel has some space to move about, but most of all be sure you lace the skates tightly but not so tightly that your feet feel imprisoned.

Since an ice rink generates cold from the ground up, always wear heavy socks that are comfortable and the right size. For those who feel frigid in their extremities, it is advisable to wear two pairs of socks so that the toes do not freeze and thus impair your ability to move about. Always be careful, after lacing, to tuck the knotted lace into the edge of the boot.

Every part of you should be covered with warm clothing. Gloves are essential, preferably the kind that is wooly on the inside, and at least one sweater should be worn. Skating outdoors can be bitingly nippy, especially for the beginner; therefore, extra care should be taken to dress warmly. Always take along a change of socks, for most probably your original pair will be soaked from skating and falling onto the ice.

Ice-skating can be a ball of fun and wonder, if you come with the right equipment and enough clothing to shield you from the cold.

Remember the steps:

1. Outline the main ideas.

2. List them in the order of happening.

3. Reduce the wording to about half.

Now write your summary.

HOW DO I WRITE A RESUME LETTER TO APPLY FOR A JOB?

SALES
MGMT ASST   CALL STUDENTS
Summer Jobs
Immediate openings in Business Product Service Division of large national publishing co. calling only on businesses. Base salary + commissions averaging $250 weekly income. No experience nec. Full training. For appointment contact Bell Agency, 475 Fifth Ave.

LIFE GUARDS—EXPERIENCED
Must be over 17 years — Must have all necessary credentials including Red Cross card.
162-15 Smith St., Jamaica

COUNSELORS
Athletic, WSI, tennis. Res girls camp, Southhampton NY. ALSO coed camp Penna. Write:
Camp Arrow
Southhampton, N.Y.

If you were interested in one of these openings, how would you go about applying for the job?

What should a letter of application contain?

ASSIGNMENT

BOOKKEEPER — Bright, Conscientious, Cooperative, for pleasant midtown office. Sales and purchase experience preferred. Salary open. Must be capable of assisting in running office. Send résumé.
MM416 TIMES

You see an advertisement in the newspaper for a job that suits you perfectly. You are excited by the prospects of having this job, and you are certain you have the qualifications and can do the job well. The ad, in addition to describing the job, asks that you send in a résumé. How do you go about writing a résumé?

A résumé is a description of your background with regard to schooling, employment, activities you have participated in, honors and awards you may have won, and services you have performed. Simply, it is a summary that tells the employer all the basic facts about your life that will help him judge whether or not you are a good candidate for the job. On the basis of the résumé letter that you write, you will or will not be called upon for an interview. That depends on how well you write the résumé.

Since this is the very first impression an employer will have of you, your résumé letter should be *neat*, *well organized*, and *thorough*. Include only those facts that relate to the job description and that build up a good case for you. Other information that does not apply may result in rejection.

Points to Remember

NEATNESS:

Sloppy, illegible writing is a reflection of one's character. If you dash off a résumé letter that shows no care or consideration for neatness, why should the person reading it (usually the personnel manager) bother to consider you? Chances are, since this person has hundreds of other, neater letters to read, your letter will be tossed into the basket. Typing a letter of application, obviously, has advantages, since it creates a tone of formality which is proper in business circles.

ORGANIZATION:

How you put your ideas together is crucial. A résumé letter that is poorly arranged, in which one idea does not follow logically from another, is another indication of an attitude that will turn off an employer. Generally, there is a widely accepted way to organize ideas in a résumé.

Paragraph 1: State specifically the job you are applying for, where and when you saw the classified ad, and why you believe you should be considered.

Paragraph 2: Describe your background — other jobs you have held, successes in school that apply to the job, people who know you and can write good references about you, other related experiences in business. Certain facts about you — your age, your address and telephone number, how far you have gone in school, whether or not you have working papers, your social security number — should be included.

Paragraph 3: This part is a complimentary close. Here you end the letter by courteously expressing a deep interest in securing the position, reemphasizing how well-prepared you think you are, and where and when you can be reached. (It is not necessary to mention salary unless you are requested to do so.)

Procedure

STEP 1: READ THE AD AND UNDERSTAND IT

This is essential, for applying for a job for which you are not qualified is a waste of your time as well as that of the company. You must read the ad over and over until you understand every word. Then you must ask yourself: "Am I well qualified for the position described in this ad?" If yes, then you are ready for the next step.

STEP 2: PLAN BACKGROUND DESCRIPTIONS

This is the substance of your résumé letter; it contains all the vital data about you. This is the part the employer will study carefully to see if you have the required background. On a piece of paper, list the following categories:

1. Education

2. Actual jobs held

3. Neighborhood activities

4. Awards and honors won

5. Other related experiences

6. People who will write references for me

Next to each item, make a list of the information that applies. For example, the area "Actual Jobs Held" may look something like this:

Actual Jobs Held

1. I worked as assistant bookkeeper in the summer of 1974, in Camp Merrimac, Contoocook, New Hampshire.
2. After school and on weekends, I work in my father's factory, Springfield Corporation, 555 Fifth Avenue, New York, helping the head bookkeeper prepare payrolls.
3. In my school, Martin Van Buren High School, 232 Street and Hillside Avenue, Queens Village, New York, I have given service in the school treasurer's office, where I have learned how to record expenditures for school activities.

In this way, you do the same for each other item. Remember, this is only an outline to help you in the final writing. Once you have all the facts needed to construct an impressive résumé, then you are ready for the actual writing.

STEP 3: WRITE YOUR LETTER

If you were to type your letter of application, it should look something like this:

> 63-31 Jason Avenue
> Jamaica, New York 11435
>
> July 30, 1979

Box MM416
New York Times
229 West 43rd Street
New York, N.Y. 10036

Dear Sir:

In reply to your advertisement for a bookkeeper in the July 18 Sunday *New York Times*, I am enclosing for your consideration a résumé of my qualifications for the position. On the basis of my experience and work background, I believe I am well-qualified for the position you wish to fill.

At Martin Van Buren High School, the school from which I just graduated, I pursued a commercial course, which taught me all the essentials of bookkeeping practice. In each class I received at least an 85 for the term. During my free period each day, I assisted the school treasurer in recording and filing school expenditures. At graduation I was awarded a certificate of excellence in bookkeeping. In the summer of 1974, I was hired by the owner of Camp Merrimac, Contoocook, New Hampshire, to work as an assistant bookkeeper in the business office and there I learned more complex procedures. In my father's factory, located at 555 Fifth Avenue, New York, N.Y., I worked with the head bookkeeper in preparing payrolls. In the neighborhood Democratic Club, where I volunteer time, I help in keeping records of contributions made and expenses for publicity. I have enrolled in Nassau Community College, Garden City, New York, for an associate degree in business administration.

The following people have indicated they are available as references:

Mr. Werner Rothschild, owner of Camp Merrimac, Contoocook, New Hampshire 03229

Mrs. May Lind, school treasurer, Martin Van Buren High School, 232 Street and Hillside Avenue, Queens Village, New York 11427

Mrs. Jane Putney, head bookkeeper, Springfield Corporation, 555 Fifth Avenue, New York, N.Y. 10017

I am available for an interview and can be reached at (212) SP 6-4729.

If there are further particulars you wish, please contact me at the above address. Thank you for your time and consideration of me for the position of assistant bookkeeper in your firm.

Respectfully yours,

Roland Smith

STEP 4: REVISE

After you have completed the letter, read it over carefully for omissions. Ask yourself: "Have I included everything that is of importance in helping me to get the job?"

If you find you have left some important fact out, it is wise to rewrite the résumé. Remember: The letter you send them is the very first impression they have of you. The better the letter, the better the chances you have of being summoned for an interview.

Summarizing basic points: If you reread the original classified ad and then the résumé letter written in response to it, you should note the following:

1. Every letter of application for a job should be in direct response to a specific ad.
2. It should be planned first, written second.

3. It should contain only that information that pertains to the position.

4. It should follow strictly the form of a business letter — properly spaced, no abbreviations, correct margins, simply stated.

5. The organization should contain the following: Paragraph 1: which position you are applying for, the place where the ad was found. Paragraph 2: a brief outline of educational, work, and community experience. Paragraph 3: courteous closing in which you indicate your willingness to be contacted.

6. A résumé should be typed, but if you must use longhand, use your very best penmanship.

A well-written résumé does not guarantee that you will secure the job. It is merely an introduction, a way of presenting yourself excellently to an employer, so he may be impressed enough to call you for an interview. Therefore, a polished résumé enhances your chances of success.

Follow-Up Exercises

Here are several classified ads taken from newspapers for a variety of jobs. Select one you may be qualified for and compose a letter of application, as if you were seriously seeking the position.

Clerk-Typist

Marine Midland is a good place to work if you can type, handle correspondence, and perform administrative duties. Position in our insurance section offers interesting, diversified work. Experience with insurance helpful, but not an absolute.
Salary open. Send résumé to:
>   Marine Midland Bank
>   140 Broadway
>   New York, N.Y. 10015

Trainees
Material damage appraiser

If you are interested in working with automobiles and have exp in any automotive related field we have the perfect career for you. Send a résumé of related work to:
>   Geico Affiliates
>   750 Woodbury Road
>   Woodbury, N.Y. 11797

Travel Agent

Sales promotion ability. Opportunity, responsibility. Beginners with good manner and personality considered. Send résumé. X781 Times.

Assistant Buyer

Some knowledge of distribution needed, but will teach all facets of merchandising. Work directly with buyer as you learn. Send résumé.
Rainbow Shops, 756 East Orange Street, Orange, New Jersey 07615

Factory Worker

Young person skilled with hands to learn plastics/fabrics business. Good memory required. Send resume.

> Janways Industries
> Box 7208
> Oakland, California 94312

Bank Teller Trainee

Bright, well-mannered person to be schooled in all aspects of banking. Apply with resume.

> Midway Bank
> 22 Oak Street
> Chicago, Illinois 60612

HOW DO I WRITE A LETTER OF COMPLAINT?

(Credit: Bob Main. From Leo de Wys, Inc.)

What would you do if this situation existed in your town?
To whom can you complain?
How do you register this complaint?

ASSIGNMENT

Think of some situation that annoyed you so much you wanted to complain. Write a letter to a person complaining about that situation.

How do you do this?

Very often we are disappointed or dissatisfied with the way a person treats us or with a purchase we make that is not quite what it was represented to be. We know how we feel in these frustrating situations, but do we know what to do about them? Do we know how to respond in such a way that the annoyance is corrected? The answer lies in knowing how to compose a letter that describes the situation in such a convincing way that the person to whom it is addressed will respond in a satisfying way.

Example

A student receives a program at the beginning of the term and is shocked to see a change she never requested. The fact of the matter is that it is an error. She is so annoyed that she goes to see her advisor about it but can't get an interview because there is a long line of other students with similar problems. So, in anger, she puts this letter together:

November 16, 1979

Dear Mrs. Greenfield,

That's really a rotten way to treat me, your changing my program from an English to a math class. I'm so upset and angry I could scream. Now I have to suffer through another math class, which I don't need and which I hate. I've got to see you right away so you can clear up this mess.

An angry student,

Mary Stoke

This is a poor letter that will not get results. Can you see why?

1. It is written in an angry tone.

2. It doesn't explain the problem clearly.

3. No specific facts are given.

4. It antagonizes the reader instead of convincing.

5. The form — the way it is put together — is poor.

How, then, do you write a letter of complaint for a situation like this?

November 16, 1979

Dear Mrs. Greenfield:

I wish to bring to your attention how distressed I am with the way you switched my English 56 class to Math 54. The truth is I chose not to continue with math last term, and at the conference we had then you indicated you would note that on my record. Obviously there is an error that must be corrected at once.

Kindly indicate when I can see you to take up this matter of changing my program to the original one.

Sincerely yours,

Mary Stoke

How is this second letter better than the first? This letter is courteous and more formal in tone. It clearly explains the girl's problem. The facts of the classes are given. It alerts the reader to an error that must be corrected. The form of the letter is sound, concise, and direct.

Example

These last five guidelines are useful in any letter of complaint you may write. Let us take, for example, another situation, one that does not involve school. A common one is automotive service. Suppose you gave your car to a service station to have the regulator and the battery changed and you find, later, that the car still does not start properly. You may return to the same station to complain, they may even attempt to fix the problem once more, but again you have trouble. What do you do?

You write a letter, one to the service station, another to the gasoline company under whose name the station operates. If it is a Texaco station, for example, you would write to the person who manages that station and a second to the Texaco company itself. Here is how it might read:

January 11, 1979

Gerald's Service Station
1190 Harold Road
Nyack, New York 12345

Dear Mr. Jones:

I wish to inform you that the battery and regulator you installed in my 1974 Ford Mustang are still not functioning efficiently. Two weeks after the job was done, on December 14, 1978, I returned with the car and you checked out the system. Your report then was that a cable was out of line. After a few days, the same trouble appeared — the car did not start and often it just conked out. When I called you to report this, you were insistent that the fault was mine, that you had done all you could. Lately, I have had my car checked out by a licensed mechanic who diagnosed the problem as a faulty regulator that you installed initially.

The cost of $80 is outrageous since the car is no better now than it was before I gave it to you. Because of your negligence and indifference, I have been advised to turn the case over to the Consumer Complaint Department of Texaco, Incorporated, as well as notify the Better Business Bureau. I have had no choice, since you continue to ignore my complaint.

It is obviously your responsibility to stand behind the work you do, and if the job is less than perfect, you are bound to follow up on the necessary repairs. Second, since you conduct your business under the name of Texaco, it seems you have a professional duty to uphold their reputation. And since you haven't, I have been compelled to take further action.

This is a distressing situation. I hope you will act quickly and efficiently to remedy the matter.

Respectfully yours,

Bill Williams

This sort of letter certainly does the following. It alerts the station to the problem; it indicates your distress in a way that doesn't offend; it gives a full picture of the trouble from the beginning; it shows you will stand behind your rights; it will get the manager of the station to act in some way.

Follow-Up Exercises

Write a letter of complaint about one of the following situations:

1. A disappointing meal in a good restaurant

2. Clothing that doesn't fit right

3. The principal's decision to cut out an activity you love

4. A politician's promise never lived up to

5. A hike in the Con Ed rates

Chapter Two

CRITICAL WRITING

In this chapter, the writing assignments require critical writing. This kind of writing involves forming an opinion and supporting your decision with details. The emphasis here is on stating a general thesis and choosing corroborating evidence to make the thesis convincing and acceptable.

The terms *critical judgment* and *point of view* may at first seem complex. All of us have a variety of views on many subjects, but only some of us have developed these views based on keen critical judgment. When we leave a movie theatre, we may hear our friends express a point of view: "That picture was terrific!" "What an exciting ending!" "He is a marvelous actor!" But this is not critical judgment. To judge a movie critically, the writer must take a point of view and support it with strong evidence or reasons. Critical judgment regarding a movie, for example, must go beyond the expression "terrific" to specific reasons *why* you feel the picture was outstanding, such as its special effects, some acting techniques, or unique camera shots.

HOW DO I WRITE A LITERATURE ESSAY ANSWER FOR A TEST?

ASSIGNMENT

Novels deal with people and their conflicts, the ways in which individuals or groups deal with problems. Sometimes these conflicts are resolved by the person, at other times they are not. Using a novel you have read this term, write an essay stating specifically what you consider to be the chief conflict, how the character is affected by it, and how successfully it is resolved.

How do you do this?

STEP 1: READ THE QUESTION TO UNDERSTAND DIRECTIONS

The secret here is focusing on the area about which you will write. If you read the question carefully, you will note the word is *conflict*. (A conflict may be a problem.) But it must be a problem an individual or a group of individuals face.

STEP 2: THINK OF THE RIGHT CHOICE

Obviously, the book you choose must have a conflict, a person or persons dealing with it, and some resolution of this problem. If you see this focus clearly, you will not make the mistake of using a novel that is inappropriate.

STEP 3: MAKE A DECISION

Let us say, for instance, you read George Orwell's *1984*, a great satirical novel that tries to warn us of the dangers of the future. Ask yourself: "What conflicts are treated in this book?"

STEP 4: OUTLINE POSSIBILITIES

Of course it is possible that a novel may have a number of conflicts. But you must decide which is the most important one, the one developed throughout the entire story. First make a list of those that come to mind:

1. Oceania rules its people with an iron hand.

2. Big Brother watches the actions of all people.

3. The Thought Police even read people's minds.

4. Human love is outlawed and forbidden.

5. The Inner Party is the privileged class.

Ask yourself: "In what way is each a problem, who is the character involved, how does he deal with it, and to what extent is he successful in resolving it?"

STEP 5: MAKE A DECISION

Item 4 of the possibilities deals with a problem that two characters in the book are suddenly caught up with. The government of Oceania (Ingsoc) forbids anything resembling romance or love. Even sex has lost its passionate meaning. Julia and Winston, two party workers, are attracted to each other and fall in love. Secretly, they meet and make love. They know that what they are doing is dangerous and against the law, but they are willing to take the chance. This is a perfect conflict because it concerns an individual's choice in relation to the society in which he lives.

STEP 6: OUTLINE THE ANSWER

Go back to the original question and note the parts. You are asked specifically what you consider to be the chief conflict, how the character is affected by it, and how successfully it is overcome.

1. State the conflict.

2. Name the character and show how he or she is affected.

3. Is the conflict overcome? If so, how?

STEP 7: SUPPORT A GENERALIZATION WITH A SPECIFIC REFERENCE

In the outline indicate scenes in the book that illustrate your ideas. For example, Part 2 should read:

2. The character and how he or she is affected.
Winston is attracted to Julia and refuses to give her up.

Example: When he first sights Julia in the Ministry of Truth, they stare at each other secretly.

Example: Though it is a crime, they meet in the woods and make love.

Example: Winston rents a room from Mr. Charrington as a rendezvous.

Example: Winston and Julia agree their relationship is an act of defiance against the state.

STEP 8: ORGANIZE THE ANSWER

With these concrete examples to support your statement of the conflict, you should make a decision as to whether or not Winston overcomes the problem successfully. Part 3 should read:

3. Is the conflict overcome? The problem is resolved when they are caught in the act of love.

Example: The telescreen lights up and a voice shouts at them.

Example: Mr. Charrington is really a party member who attempts to cure Winston.

Statement: The conflict of Winston's individual action against the wishes of the state is resolved by torture and conversion to party thinking. It was a futile act of rebellion.

STEP 9: WRITE THE LITERATURE ESSAY

The language you use should be simple, clear, and direct. This is not a creative paper but an interpretive one. Therefore, you should deal only with the events of the story as they apply to your definition of conflict.

If you follow the steps outlined in this chapter, your answer should read somewhat as follows:

> The main conflict in the novel *1984*, by George Orwell, is the attempt of an individual citizen of a state to resist the law. By setting the story in the future, the author more vividly illustrates the futility of defiance against a government that denies its people not only basic freedoms but natural desires.
>
> Winston, a worker in the Ministry of Truth, is the character who represents a rebellious spirit. This rebelliousness is shown in the form of love that he feels toward another party worker, Julia. From the very moment he sets eyes on her, he is physically attracted, but such attractions are forbidden. Therefore, their flirtation must continue secretly. When they pass each other in the cafeteria, Julia hands him a note which tells him where and when to meet, in a place where Big Brother will not observe them. There, in the woods, they make love and relate passionately to each other. It is dangerous but they are determined to hold on to the one thing they hold dear — human love. Thus, Winston rents an out-of-the-way room in Mr. Charrington's antique shop where Julia and he meet as often as possible. Their love grows to a point of defiance because they know their relationship is a cardinal sin in Oceania. But they have no choice: They must continue to meet despite the danger.
>
> The conflict comes to a head when guards burst into their room and a thunderous voice on the telescreen orders them to freeze. They are arrested and punished severely for their crime. In a long scene involving interrogation

by O'Brien, who Winston thought was a member of the Brotherhood but who is in reality a high official in the inner party, we see how the state psychologically reforms, or brainwashes, its prisoners. Winston resists at first, but through a series of indescribable tortures and abuses he is converted back to a model citizen and his whole notion of individual acts of will is eliminated.

The conflict of Winston's action against the wishes of the state is resolved by torture and ultimate conversion to party thinking. As it turns out, a person's resistance against a dictatorship like Oceania is a futile act of rebellion. It is obvious that George Orwell believed that if we don't change our ways we will reach a stage when all personal rights and freedoms are not only denied but actually eliminated.

STEP 10: EVALUATION

Now read over the paper completely to see whether the answer satisfies the original question. Is there a conflict? Is there a character involved in the conflict? Is the conflict in some way resolved? Remember these points:

1. Read the question carefully.

2. Underline key words.

3. Try to understand the focus of the question.

4. Select the right piece of literature to answer the question.

5. Compose an outline first.

6. Support every statement with an example from the book.

7. Do not summarize the story.

8. Put ideas together clearly, directly, and simply.

9. Always reread the paper for possible revisions.

Follow-Up Exercise

Write a literature essay for the following question, using a novel, play, or biography you have read this year:

In literature as in life people are forced to make decisions. Sometimes the decisions turn out for the good, while at other times they turn out for the worse. Select a book or a play you have read and (1) state the decision the person makes and (2) explain whether this decision was a good or bad one.

HOW DO I ANALYZE A CHARACTER?

(Credit: Arthur d'Amario. From Freelance Photographers Guild.)

Characters are people we meet in books. When we read a book, we learn about people, how they act, what they feel and think, the decisions they make, and the problems they face. In other words, we learn enough about them to *analyze*.

A character analysis, then, is a piece of writing about one particular person in a book we have read. (A character sketch, you will remember, is about a real person we know, while a character analysis depends on what we have learned from what we read.) The key to having enough to write about is to gain as much information about the person in the book as you can, so you can make some personal judgments and interpret some of his or her behavior.

If you are a reader, you should recognize many of these characters:

Adventures of Huckleberry Finn	Huck, Jim, Aunt Sally
Adventures of Tom Sawyer	Tom, Aunt Becky, Injun Joe
Anne Frank: The Diary of a Young Girl	Anne, Peter, Mr. Van Daan
The Bridge of San Luis Rey	Manuel, Uncle Pio, Marquessa
The Caine Mutiny Court Martial	Maryk, Queeg, Willy
The Call of the Wild	Buck, Spitz, François
Dr. Jekyll and Mr. Hyde	Dr. Jekyll, Mr. Utterson, Poole
The Good Earth	Wang-Lung, Olan, Lotus
Great Expectations	Joe, Pip, Miss Havisham
Kon-Tiki	Knut, Torstein, Heyerdahl
Lost Horizon	Conway, Chang, Lo-Tsen
Moby Dick	Ahab, Queequeg, Ishmael
Mutiny on the Bounty	Captain Bligh, Fletcher Christian
Of Human Bondage	Mildred, Philip
Oliver Twist	Oliver, Bill Sikes, Fagin
The Red Badge of Courage	Henry, Jim
Silas Marner	Silas, Eppie, Godfrey
A Tale of Two Cities	Madame Defarge, Lucie, Carton
Treasure Island	Jim, Long John Silver, Livesy
Wuthering Heights	Heathcliff, Catherine, Earnshaw

All of the characters in these books are well known by many readers. They have become flesh-and-blood people who think, feel, and act in ways we can relate to. They have problems they must solve, experiences from which they grow, complicated relationships with others.

ASSIGNMENT

Write a character analysis of a person in a book.

When you are ready to write a character analysis, you have to decide which person you have read about in a certain book that you wish to interpret in a certain way. The decision you make depends on the following:

1. Do you know the character well enough to say something important about him or her?

2. Are you aware of his or her struggles or conflicts?

3. Can you judge this character's actions?

4. Can you identify the problem the character is facing?

5. Do you have something original to say about him or her?

Procedure

STEP 1: CHOOSE A POINT OF VIEW

As with people you know in real life, characters in books are subject to interpretation. You may, for example, see Huck Finn as a playful, shiftless boy, while another reader may consider him a serious, curious youth. Ahab in *Moby Dick* may be perceived as an obsessive maniac, or as a very determined, single-minded individual who must find that whale no matter what. Both views may be correct depending on the selections used to support either one.

STEP 2: VALIDATE YOUR OPINION WITH A CHOICE OF PASSAGES

The secret is to underline key passages that offer evidence in support of your view. *You must always refer to the text you have read to make your analysis valid.* Otherwise you will end up with a sketch, not an analysis.

Example From Literature

Early in the play *Macbeth*, by William Shakespeare, there is a part that is very revealing of Lady Macbeth's character. From this passage alone you can draw enough evidence on which to build a character analysis.

> Glamis thou art, and Cawdor, and shalt be
> What thou art promised. Yet I do fear thy nature.
> It is too full o' the milk of human kindness
> To catch the nearest way. Thou wouldst be great;
> Art not without ambition, but without
> The illness should attend it. What thou wouldst highly,
> That wouldst thou holily; wouldst not play false.
> And yet wouldst wrongly win. Thou'ldst have, great Glamis,
> That which cries "Thus though must do, if thou have it;
> And that which rather thou dost fear to do
> Than wishest should be undone." Hie thee hither,
> That I may pour my spirits in thine ear
> And chastise with the valor of my tongue
> All that impedes thee from the golden round
> Which fate and metaphysical aid doth seem
> To have thee crowned withal.

Analysis

Lady Macbeth is a determined woman who uses any means to get her way. Now that she has been informed of her husband's success at war and his promotion, she is eager to have him succeed to the top. To do this, she will encourage him seriously to take the necessary steps. Besides being determined, she is a strong person who is willing to take risks. Knowing Macbeth is an honest, principled man who will not play false, she will try to change his nature to make him more receptive to action. Lady Macbeth is also very devoted to her husband because she wants the very best for him. Only the top will do, and she will not compromise for his sake. All in all, Lady Macbeth is the kind of woman who knows exactly what she wants and who will stop at nothing to get it.

Example From Literature

Here is another selection, this time from the book *Huckleberry Finn* by Mark Twain.

> Once I said to myself it would be a thousand times better for Jim to be a slave at home where his family was, as long as he'd got to be a slave, and so I'd better write a letter to Tom Sawyer and tell him to tell Miss Watson where he was. But I soon give up the notion for two things: she'd be mad and disgusted at his rascality and ungratefulness for leaving her, and so she'd sell him straight down the river agains; and if she didn't, everybody naturally despises an ungrateful nigger, and they'd make Jim feel it all the time, and so he'd feel ornery and disgraced. And then think of me! It would get around that Huck Finn helped a nigger to get his freedom; and if I was ever to see anybody from that town again I'd be ready to get down and lick his boots for shame. That's just the way: a person does a low-down thing, and then he don't want to take no consequences of it. Thinks as long as he can hide, it ain't no disgrace.

Analysis

Jim, a run-away slave, is traveling with Huck down the Mississippi, when it dawns on Huck that what he is doing is contrary to the rules of his society. He analyzes his situation and sees that by befriending Jim and helping him, he is not only violating the law but acting in a way that will alienate his friends and the people who know him. The thought of it frightens Huck, makes him think twice, but the reality is, as we learn later in the book, that slavery is essentially cruel and inhumane, and to return Jim to the authorities would be as barbaric as the way the slave-holders treat the blacks. Thus, in this passage, we see an innocent boy acquiring a view of the world but making his own decisions.

Points to remember about character analysis:

1. Characters in books and stories are like real people.

2. An analysis of a character should be based on judgments made from specific passages.

3. Focus on a particular trait, such as trust, kindness, honesty, or dependability.

4. Underscore this trait with reference to behavior in the text.

5. Apply the analysis of the character and his or her relationships to others, to people in real life.

6. Don't tell everything about the person. Just deal with one trait that is consistently developed.

Follow-Up Exercise

Write a character analysis of a person in a novel, short story, play, or essay you have read. Show how one quality, either bad or good, has been revealed. Apply your discussion of the quality to a specific passage or parts.

HOW DO I ANALYZE A POEM?

Life is a merry chase,
A romp through youth,
A meditation when the face is white.
The chaser soon becomes the chased.

We run away the years,
Look ahead like a plane in nose-dive,
But all it is, in this game of life,
Is a whirl toward the end.

What is the poet conveying to us *generally*?
How does he convey this idea *specifically*?

ASSIGNMENT

Write an analysis of the following poem.

I Meant to Do My Work Today

I meant to do my work today,
But a brown bird sang in the apple tree.
And a butterfly flitted across the field,
And all the leaves were calling me.

And the wind went sighing over the land,
Tossing the grasses to and fro,
And a rainbow held out its shining hand—
So what could I do but laugh and go?

by Richard Le Gallienne

Procedure

STEP 1: ANALYZE THE POEM

Read the poem several times to get a sense of the meaning. Try to state it in one sentence. When you feel you have grasped the idea of the poem, then look for specific lines, words, images, and expressions that help to convey this idea.

STEP 2: STATE THE MEANING

There may be several possible meanings to a poem, but you must decide which is the most important one for you. For example, in this particular poem you may conclude that the poet is dealing with nature and how it appeals to us, or how tempted we are to stop working hard, or how sometimes we take our responsibilities too seriously, or maybe how beautiful life can be if we would only notice. You can list these possibilities on a piece of paper:

1. Nature is very appealing to us.

2. We are always tempted to find an excuse for not working hard.

3. People tend to take their responsibilities too seriously.

4. Life is so beautiful, if we would only notice.

Now you have a decision to make by selecting one and developing this idea more fully. Suppose, for example, you consider item 4 to be the best statement of the idea of the poem. Your next step is to develop it further.

STEP 3: DEVELOP THE MAIN IDEA

Developing means explaining further. In this case, how beautiful must life be before we take notice? Now you must go back to the poem to reread it for clues. Note which lines convey the beauty of nature. What does the poet see outside his window that captures his attention? Answer: a brown bird, a butterfly flitting, the leaves calling, the wind sighing, the grass moving, and a pretty rainbow. You have enough visual evidence of how striking nature is to that man to develop a statement of this main idea.

STEP 4: A FULLER STATEMENT OF THE MAIN IDEA

The poem "I Meant To Do My Work Today," by Richard Le Gallienne, has as its main idea that life is so beautiful, if we would only notice. This idea is brought to us vividly when the poet, who is busily at work, glances out his window and is distracted by the movement of nature all around him. The birds, insects, grass, and a striking rainbow capture his attention to the point where he can no longer concentrate on his work. He is more than distracted; he is captivated.

STEP 5: SUPPORT THE MAIN IDEA

In poetry, more than in prose, language is very important in conveying a feeling about a subject. To support an idea, you must indicate examples of images that help to picture the idea. For example, "a brown bird sang in the apple tree" gives us a thrill, "a butterfly flitted across the field" provides a dancing movement, "all the leaves were calling me" personalizes the leaves as people beckoning with pleasure, while "the wind went sighing over the land" has a playful motion to it. Each image is specific, direct, and related to the idea of how beautiful nature can be, if we would only notice; in fact, so beautiful that we are inspired to leave everything to become part of that aspect of the joy of life.

STEP 6: USE SPECIFIC IMAGES TO BROADEN THE MAIN IDEA

If you go back to Step 4, the fuller statement of the main idea, you will see that the references to nature have to be pinned down more exactly. You can do this easily by referring to the lines themselves, as we did in Step 5. Here's how:

> The poet, as he looks through his window, notices a brown bird singing in the apple tree. The use of *brown* enhances our color appreciation and *singing* makes us feel the joy and sense of life that is special to this tiny creature. The apple tree apparently is a familiar place that the bird loves and appreciates. A second image that catches the poet's attention is the sudden movement of the butterfly, as in the line "And a butterfly flitted across the field," which has a dancelike effect. In addition to visions and movements, there is the use of sound, as in the line "And all the leaves were calling me," as if the leaves were humans calling the poet to join them. Another sound is caught in the line "And the wind went sighing over the land," which adds to the effect of pleasure and freedom. A sensation of light is very striking in the end of the poem, "And a rainbow held out its shining hand," which is another strong attraction that draws the writer from his work.

STEP 7: CONCLUDE THE ANALYSIS OF A POEM

As in all writing, there must be a fitting closing to the statement and the supporting details. It's a matter of rephrasing the same idea in another way. For example:

> The poet's view of nature and how beautifully it looks to us when we take the time to notice is very true. All of us get bogged down in work and become very serious, and therefore forget what it's like to be carefree and fun-loving. Nature has more than prettiness to offer us; it is an environment where we can get away from the cares of the world and just be ourselves. I suppose all of us could learn from "So what could I do but laugh and go?"

STEP 8: EVALUATION

Now we have an analysis that has a general statement supported by a variety of picture-words, followed by a conclusion which reinforces the idea. It is an acceptable way to approach a poem. Putting it all together:

The poem "I Meant To Do My Work Today," by Richard Le Gallienne, has as its main idea that life is so beautiful if we would only notice. This idea is brought to us vividly when the poet, who is busily at work, glances out his window and is distracted by the movements of nature all around him. The birds, insects, grass, and a striking rainbow capture his attention to the point where he can no longer concentrate on his work. He is more than distracted; he is captivated.

The poet, as he looks through his window, notices a brown bird singing in the apple tree. The use of *brown* enhances our color appreciation and *singing* makes us feel the joy and sense of life that is special to this tiny creature. The apple tree apparently is a familiar place that the bird loves and appreciates. A second image that catches the poet's attention is the sudden movement of the butterfly, as in the line "And a butterfly flitted across the field," which has a dancelike effect. In addition to visions and movements, there is the use of sound, as in the line "And all the leaves were calling me," as if the leaves were humans calling the poet to join them. Another sound is caught in the line "And the wind went sighing over the land," which adds to the effect of pleasure and freedom. A sensation of light is very striking in the end of the poem, "And a rainbow held out its shining hand," which is another strong attraction that draws the writer from his work.

The poet's view of nature and how beautifully it looks when we take the time to notice is true. All of us are bogged down in work and become very serious, and therefore forget what it's like to be carefree and fun-loving. Nature has more than prettiness to offer us; it is an environment where we can get away from the cares of the world and just be ourselves. I suppose all of us could learn from "So what could I do but laugh and go?"

Now you have a poem analysis you can be proud of. These are important guidelines to remember:

1. Read a poem several times until you *feel* its meaning for you.

2. Decide on one principal meaning and state it in one sentence.

3. Develop this one-sentence meaning by explaining key words.

4. Reread the poem to find support for your main idea.

5. Select images (word-pictures) that expand the meaning.

6. Refer to each one in your analysis, quoting exact lines.

7. Conclude the analysis by restating the opening idea in an original way.

8. Always stick to the one idea you have chosen.

9. Reread your paper to determine whether you have answered the question, to be sure you are organized, and to correct language errors.

Follow-Up Exercise

Read the following poem very carefully to determine the main idea. State it fully, support it with references in the poem, and make a final conclusion.

Sea Fever

I must go down to the seas again, to the lonely sea and the sky,
And all I ask is a tall ship and a star to steer her by,
And the wheel's kick and the wind's song and the white sail's shaking,
And a gray mist on the sea's face and a gray dawn breaking.

I must go down to the seas again, for the call of the running tide
Is a wild call and clear call that may not be denied;
And all I ask is a windy day with the white clouds flying,
And the flung spray and the blown spume, and the sea gulls crying.

I must go down to the seas again, to the vagrant gypsy life.
To the gull's way and the whale's way where the wind's like a whetted knife;
And all I ask is a merry yarn from a laughing fellow rover,
And quiet sleep and a sweet dream when the long trick's over.

by John Masefield

HOW DO I WRITE A BOOK REPORT?

(Credit: Leo de Wys, Inc.)

How do you choose a book for a book report?
How would you review your favorite book?

The book report is the most basic kind of writing in all English classes. Your teacher will usually assign a book to be read by a certain time, then ask you to write something about it. The writing may be called a *report*, a *review*, or an *interpretation*. The teacher expects you to have read the book and to be able to communicate something that you feel is important about it.

ASSIGNMENT

You have just completed reading a full-length novel (discussed in class), and now your teacher writes on the board: "Compose a 300-word report on the novel we have just finished."

How do you go about writing this report?

Procedure

STEP 1: THINK ABOUT WHAT YOU WANT TO SAY

A book report has to say something important about a main character, his or her life, the decisions he or she has to make, the experiences, the relationships with other people, and the changes that come about in his or her life. You must first think about the book as a whole and then decide what is most revealing about a main character and that person's life.

STEP 2: DECIDE ON THE MOST IMPORTANT AREA OF THE BOOK

After you have answered the question "What is this book telling me about this character and his or her life?" it is wise to write down on a piece of paper a clear, concise answer to that question. For example, let us say your book is about war and how a soldier experiences the realities of modern warfare. This, you decide, is the most outstanding point about the book. Therefore, write on a piece of paper: "The novel I have read, _____ by _____, shows the struggles of a young man trying to adapt to the horrors of war." Study this line and think of ways to develop it further.

STEP 3: DEVELOP THE BASIC THEME

What you have written on your paper is known as a statement of theme. The theme is the overriding idea that runs through the entire book. But to develop a theme statement you need to explain and clarify. For this you must deal with the key words in the theme and expand on them. If you look back at our original statement, you will note that the words *struggles*, *adapt*, and *horrors* are the three key words. Therefore, they must be developed further. Next you should describe the particular struggles, how well the character adapted, and just how horrible war is.

STEP 4: EXPAND ON KEY WORDS

On your paper, write the word *struggle* in one column, the word *adapt* in another, and the word *horrible* in a third. Under each, write at least three examples from the book that illustrate each word. For example, the character in his first experience with battle might discover the agony and suffering of his buddies. Later, he may discover that being a soldier is like being a machine, without any personal identity. Still another struggle may be with war itself. He may ask why countries start them and send so many lives to be destroyed. You now have three solid illustrations of the struggles of a young soldier. Your outline, now, should look something like this:

The novel I have read, _____ by _____, shows the struggles of a young man to adapt to the horrors of war.

Struggles
1. War is agony and suffering.
2. Soldiers are trained to be machines and to obey orders.
3. Wars are a stupid and useless way of solving problems.

Naturally, you proceed in the same manner with the words *adapt* and *horrible*.

STEP 5: USE THE BOOK AS SPECIFIC REFERENCE

Now that you have a framework for developing this book report, you must go one step further and focus on specific scenes in the book that pinpoint your ideas. Still dealing with the word *struggle*, you must ask yourself: "Where in the book are there examples of how war is agony and suffering, how soldiers are molded into machines, and how futile such destruction is?" Finding the exact page where these situations occur is not important; what is more important is that you refer to a particular scene in the book that supports your general statement. So here you must rely on memory. If you can find the exact part of the book where the scene occurs, you may wish to reread the part to refresh your memory.

STEP 6: REFER TO THE SCENE ACCURATELY

Obviously you must know what you are talking about, and the best way to prove to your teacher that you have read the book well is to include accurate information about these key scenes. Let us say the main character, early in the book, witnesses his first battle and his buddies are dying all around him. In still another scene, later in the book, he passes a number of corpses and is "struck dumb" by the sight. "Struck dumb" is the phrase actually used by the author and, if you can, it is wise to quote such phrases. Perhaps in another section of the book, the young soldier sees a village razed and innocent citizens massacred. To make your book report substantial and convincing, you must refer to these passages. Doing so will show you have read with intelligence and understanding.

STEP 7: EXPAND THE OUTLINE TO INCLUDE SPECIFICS

By now your column for the word *struggles* should look like this:

Struggles

1. War is agony and suffering.

Illustration 1: In the early part of the book the character is rushed to the front to defend a position. While he fires into the enemy, he hears the screams of dying and wounded men. He is frightened but he holds his ground.

Illustration 2: After this battle, while heading toward another position, he files by "the corpses of men that lay stretched like logs in a woodland."

Illustration 3: Against his will, he is commanded to attack a strategic village, where "men, but especially women and children, fall like fish into nets." He is appalled but fires mercilessly like the others.

And so you proceed, culling illustrations for your other specific statements of *struggle*, listing them under "Soldiers are trained to be machines and to obey orders" and "War is a stupid and useless way of solving problems." Your outline, too, should contain similar information for your other two key words, *adapt* and *horrors*.

When you have done all this, then you are on your way to writing a book report that will have some insight and skill.

STEP 8: PUT THEMATIC IDEAS TOGETHER COHERENTLY

Now you are ready to put everything together—your general thematic statement, your subdivision, your illustrations—in an organized, coherent way. The trick is to fit it all together so that the writing holds tightly and relates to one unifying idea, the one you started with: "The novel I have read, _____ by _____, conveys the struggles of a young man to adapt to the horrors of war."

How do you do this?

Rule 1: Stick only to the theme idea.

Rule 2: Don't get carried away by other, irrelevant ideas.

Rule 3: Never, never be tempted to tell the story. Your teacher no doubt knows the plot of the book. What he or she wants to read is an analysis, not a summary.

Rule 4: Paragraph for each new step. For example, when you have covered all the many struggles the hero has, then you are ready to begin a new paragraph and deal with the ways he adapts to his surroundings.

Rule 5: Use smooth transitions from one idea to another. Such words as *for example*, *for instance*, *however*, *in addition*, and *later* are useful bridges between thoughts.

STEP 9: REVISE THE REPORT

This is as important as anything else you do in writing a book report. Think of it as looking into a mirror after you are fully dressed to be sure everything is in place. Check for spelling, usage, grammatical structure, sentence order, paragraphing, originality of language, and accuracy. But also ask yourself, "Does what I have written all relate to my opening thematic statement?"

A Model Book Report

As an example of how an acceptable book report should look, the following analysis of Stephen Crane's *The Red Badge of Courage* should serve to remind you of all the basic ingredients of writing this chapter has dealt with. Read it carefully and see if you can identify the rules you have been taught.

The novel *The Red Badge of Courage* by Stephen Crane deals with the struggles of a young recruit in the Union army to adapt to the horrors of war. He is very romantic about war, thinking that being a soldier is the way to become a hero. After he enters the Civil War and is sent to the front, he sees the ugly reality: that war destroys human lives and makes many men miserable. He soon finds that he has to struggle not only to stay alive but to understand the forces that make men fight one another.

One such struggle is getting accustomed to the agony that war causes. Henry Fleming, our boy hero, has always thought of wars as games of adventure, without seeing the bloodshed. Therefore, entering the army is like a sport he is playing, but he soon discovers the rules are different. For example, after waiting impatiently with his men for marching orders, he is directed to move toward a key position. On the way, he sees ranks of wounded filing by with shock and fear written on their faces. Later, the first corpse he notices on the ground draws his attention to the face. The dead man looks so peaceful, as if asleep. More horrible still is the sight of his own best friend Jim dying before his eyes. At last, war has come to him in its full tragic way.

Still another struggle Henry faces is accepting himself as a robot designed to follow orders blindly. War, as described by the author, is a giant machine that grips men in its movements. Henry soon realizes he is just one of a thousand nameless, insignificant ranks of blue. In his first encounter with the enemy, for example, he is commanded by the lieutenant to stand and fight, but he is tempted to flee for his life. However, out of fear, he remains. Soon, the enemy charge across the field causes panic along the line, and before he knows it, Henry is one of many running for his life. It is only after he awakens to his cowardice that he can be himself again, and the rest of the book is an attempt to undo this momentary cowardice.

Perhaps the greatest struggle he faces is accepting that waging war is a futile, senseless way of solving difference. Even at the end, after he becomes a hero, he wonders, "Is this what all these men have died for?" He has emerged from the horrors of war a hero, has found his manhood again, but he is scarred forever by the exposure to the destructive machine that feeds men to their death. In addition, the battles of American against American seem to him stupid.

Henry Fleming, now a veteran, has endured butchery and massacre, but at a great cost. For one thing, he has lost the innocence of boyhood and has taken on the experience of manhood. For another, he has seen such ugly scenes of physical and mental suffering that he can never forget. Finally, he can no longer be the dreamer he was as a child. Life is too grim now, too heavy with grief.

Analysis

Does this serve as a satisfactory book report? The answer is yes. It states an overriding theme, develops it, offers examples, and is coherently organized. It flows well, and has smooth transitions; and the language conveys a deeper sense of what the book is about.

It is also the kind of book report that shows analysis and independent thinking, not just a superficial rehash of the story. The student here has given a view of the novel that is forceful, insightful, and perceptive.

You too can do the same for any book you read. Just remember the rules of thinking, planning, and writing.

Follow-Up Exercises

Consider any book, play, or short story you have read recently. Think of these skeletal areas first:

1. The theme (the overall idea)

2. Development of the thematic idea

3. Specific examples of the theme

   Example a:

   Example b:

   Example c:

4. Conclusion

   Write approximately two hundred words focusing on this one area and develop it smoothly and effectively.

HOW DO I WRITE A MOVIE REVIEW?

(Credit: United Press International.)

ASSIGNMENT

See a current movie playing in your neighborhood and write a review of it.

How do you do this?

Everybody goes to the movies, it seems, to be entertained, but how many go to study movies as works of art? That is what movie reviewing involves: seeing a film as more than an adventure or escape vehicle. It is, in many ways, seeing it as a book, or a painting, or a piece of sculpture — in other words, as a work of art.

Actually, most movies mirror life. Like books, they focus on people and the problems of life. The major difference is that, in the movies, life unfolds on a screen. It is a reality, nevertheless. Look for the following in a movie:

1. Theme

2. Artistic focus

3. Realism or fantasy

4. Conflict

5. Characterization

6. Acting

7. Dialogue

8. Film techniques

9. Scenery

10. Musical background

The problem with reviewing a movie is that you are seated in the dark and thus cannot take notes. Therefore, you have to rely on memory, but if you train your eye to see more than the story, you can retain a lot of information that would be useful in composing a review. For example, consider the movie *The Front*, starring Woody Allen. It is a bold film that tries to capture those frightful days of the early 1950s when so many artists were blacklisted because they were accused of being Communists. Because they refused to testify, or avoided the questions of the House Un-American Activities Committee, they lost their jobs and were never employed again.

Or, you can deal with the character Woody Allen plays, a front man for blacklisted writers who collects fees for their scripts. In the process of deceiving others, he gets caught up in personal greed and public conscience. Woody, a comic actor of great talent, plays this part somewhat seriously and thus makes us believe that there are people who, when others are down, will take advantage to gain something for themselves.

Thus we have identified two key elements worth reviewing in *The Front* — theme and characterization.

If you were going to review the film *The Exorcist*, you would probably deal with the fantastic effects used to convey the devil. So convincing are these special effects that the audience is shocked and horrified. You yourself don't have to believe in such evil forces, but watching the movie certainly makes you aware of their possible existence.

In the film *Rocky* your attention would be focused chiefly on a good-hearted fighter striving to make it in a tough world. The odds are against him but he never loses his decency. The *conflict*, or struggle, he faces is that of a man in his thirties battling to be a success in a world that works against him. Thus tension builds as we see him rise to that great moment, the big fight. We support him all the way because he is a symbol of the little man against the powers-that-be. How do you put a movie review together?

Procedure

STEP 1: WATCH THE MOVIE CAREFULLY

Go to the movies with an observant eye, not just to be entertained. An observant eye means looking for strengths and weaknesses in a film.

STEP 2: RECORD YOUR OBSERVATIONS IN A NOTEBOOK AFTER THE FILM IS OVER

Write down what you liked or disliked about the film immediately, as there is a tendency to forget your first impressions.

STEP 3: LOOK FOR A CENTRAL FOCUS

As in books, films do have a "center." It may be a larger theme about people and how they face life or a more specific development of a character and how he or she develops. Sometimes the focus may be an issue that is current and vital, such as crime in the streets, the values of the young generation, or the corruption of government. You have to train yourself to grasp an issue when it is there before you.

STEP 4: NOTICE TECHNICAL ASPECTS

Note the technical aspects of the film, such as the musical background, the scenery, the lighting, the acting, the use of the camera. You should be able to explain how each is effectively conveyed technically.

STEP 5: CONSIDER THE GOOD AND BAD POINTS

Comment on what you perceive to be the positive aspects of the film. Support them with examples. Then refer to the negative ones, those you perceive as weakening the film. In other words, a good movie review is a balance of both good and bad points.

The Ritz is a hilarious spoof of the bathhouses that operate in all major cities mainly for the benefit of gay men. Through a series of wacky episodes, the film gives us a caricature of males on the make. Through the eyes of one ordinary character who mistakenly gets mixed up in this atmosphere, we get a clear picture of the comedy that exists behind these closed doors. As he avoids all the bids for his favors, very funny incidents take place, and we laugh at the commonplaceness of it all.

All the characters, except for the central one, are on the fringes of our society, and they are played to the hilt. But it is Chita Rivera, a dynamite entertainer, who carries the film forward to a very entertaining close. As an actress on the make for the big role, she is the only woman among all the men, and what happens to her can put you in stitches.

Through outlandish costumes and close-ups that show you the silliness of this life in the baths, the producers of this merry romp capture absurdity. Through the use of creative lighting effects in the night club scene, the director quite effectively conveys the secrecy of male companionship.

It is not a film for all — certainly not for the overly squeamish or moral — but for those who don't mind uncovering what lies beneath the surface of our society. As such, this movie presents truth in the guise of comedy. Besides, it has enough silliness to make any sober person smile at the ridiculousness of people taking their pleasures.

Analysis

What is good about this review of *The Ritz*? If you read the review carefully, you will note it covers the following:

1. An idea of what the movie is about

2. The seriousness behind the comedy

3. The kinds of roles the actors play

4. Costumes and lighting effects

5. Which people would benefit most from seeing the film

This is what a movie review should do: cover a number of important areas of the film that a reader may want to know before making a decision whether or not to see it. Variety is the key to movie reviewing.

Important reminder: You may mention what the story is about, but never review a film for the story alone.

HOW DO I WRITE AN EDITORIAL?

Every day there is mention in your newspaper of a gasoline shortage. One day, you say, there will be enough gasoline. Yet, for a variety of reasons, this day just doesn't come. Long line-ups at pumps, soaring prices, shorter hours of distribution all contribute to the confusion.

The most sensible way to stabilize the situation is to ration gasoline fairly. In that way we won't have to stand in long lines wasting time the way we did in 1974. Research shows that if gasoline were rationed, each automobile could have 53 gallons per month, and therefore consumption would be reduced by 20%, more than enough to cover the present shortage. On 53 gallons, most people would be able to travel to their jobs and even have some gallons left for weekend travel. Of course, people with special problems could appeal for additional supplies.

Instead of waiting interminably on lines, the American public could bring their cars to gas stations in a more intelligent fashion: every other day, for example. Such a system — odds and evens — would work if the drivers of this nation took the problem seriously enough and did not panic.

Rationing is the only sane way to solve this nationwide dilemma. Instead of blaming oil-producing countries, or our own leaders, for mismanagement, let's look at ourselves and our sometimes indiscriminate use of our natural resources.

What do you call this kind of writing?

Why is it written?

Can you write something like this?

An editorial is a newspaper article (usually written by an editor) that gives an opinion on a certain subject. Every newspaper has an editorial section for that purpose.

News articles tell of actual events (crime, war, government) with facts. Newspaper reporters must write without giving their opinions. The editorial is the place where the writer can express his opinions and feelings. An editorial may tell certain basic facts about a situation but it also shows how the writer reacts to those facts.

Example

As you read this newspaper editorial, separate the facts from the opinions, the objective truth as compared to the subjective.

Planes in Beirut

The first civil airliners since last June landed at Beirut airport this weekend. Both symbolically and practically, the landings represented the nearest approach to normal conditions that the tortured city has seen in a long time.

For Lebanon as a whole, the Syrian occupation — now nearly complete — seems to have effectively stopped the civil war, at least for the time being. The Palestinians, the Christians and the other factions among the Lebanese inhabitants still nurture their hatreds and mutual suspicions, but all have surrendered to the corporate decision of the most influential Arab nations — particularly Saudi Arabia — that the fighting must stop and that the Syrians must be trusted as relatively neutral troops who at the least can end the killing.

But each day of comparative quiet in the new Lebanon makes more urgent the larger question of peace and the future in the Middle East. Will the Syrians try to destroy the belt of friendly Christian-dominated territory the Israelis have helped set up in southern Lebanon near their border? Will the Palestinians resume raids against Israel from Lebanon, and if so how will Jerusalem respond? Do the Syrians intend to annex Lebanon or is their occupation just a genuine short-term expedient that Lebanese President Sarkis can end by ordering Syrian troops out of his country when he deems conditions suitable?

Merely to ask these questions is to underline how much remains undetermined in Lebanon and in the wider Arab-Israeli confrontation. But at least the restoration of a precarious peace in Lebanon is a reminder that constant killings among different religions and ideologies are not necessarily an inevitable feature of life in the Middle East, that most sensitive area of this planet.

Notice how this editor takes the basic facts of the civil war in Beirut, Lebanon — the intervention of the Syrian army, the Middle East situation in general — and raises some questions of his own. If you map it out, you can see how logical the organization is.

Paragraph 1:   The establishment of peace (facts)

Paragraph 2:   The restoration of order by Syria (facts)

Paragraph 3:   The editor's questions which express his own concern (opinions)

Paragraph 4:   The seriousness of the situation (opinion)

Example

Look at your own school newspaper and you will undoubtedly find an editorial section. Here is an example of one in which an editor expresses a personal view.

Crowded Corner

By Mindy Wolin

The din in the hall was unbearable. Most of the noise came from people grunting, "Shush! be quiet; we're gonna get kicked out." Crammed inside the four-by-twenty foot office there were approximately 30 or 40 people. Unfortunately some wretches were forced to stand on the floor: we, the more fortunate ones, perched in choice positions on the furniture.

CB 54B is the cozy little home of two of Van Buren's major publications — The Bee Line and Futura. Owing to programming complications and mix-ups, and budgetary fate, the staffs of both Bee Line and Futura have been compelled to cohabit the same limited office space.

During the seventh period when both staffs merge, the room resembles the pornographic corner of Times Square, hardly conducive to accomplishing creative tasks. Despite our pleas for a sanctuary of our own, the Futura and Bee Line staffs seem doomed to room together.

We understand the fiscal difficulties that the administration faces and the other assorted problems they are confronted with. Still, in the hope of continuing our publications on the same level of excellence which is our tradition, we ask for a home of our own. We hope our requests will not be taken in vain and that some action is taken.

The reality of cramped space comes through in this editorial. The writer takes the truth of a serious school problem and underscores it humorously by indicating (1) there is no place even to stand or sit, (2) the crowdedness you would expect on a busy corner, and (3) the fear of being evicted if the students or the staff make too much noise.

Note: This is an effective editorial because it exposes a situation that the writer thinks should be remedied.

LETTERS TO THE EDITOR

Although you may never have the opportunity to head a staff of writers and thus have your own editorial column, nevertheless you have the opportunity to write newspapers expressing your strong views on issues. Perhaps you have a point of view you feel should be known. What do you do? Most editorial pages have a section called "Letters to the Editor" to which readers send personal comments and opinions. Newspapers welcome honest, sincere commentary from their readers even though they may not agree. This is called democratic journalism.

Here is an example from a newspaper of one letter to the editor:

> I just have to write to express my horror at the killing of animals. Hunting is the cruelest of sports, a savage display of man's inhumanity to other living creatures.
>
> How long will we tolerate this destruction of poor innocent animals who have no chance against man's long arm — the gun? How long will we justify such a disgraceful indifference to God's creations? I wonder why hunters, in particular, lust after flesh in this manner.
>
> There are reasons enough. Some men find pleasure in inflicting pain on others. It is a way of venting frustrations, failures, and discontent with life. Their pleasures, unfortunately, are society's pains.
>
> So what can we do? We can certainly write to our legislators demanding tougher laws against the wholesale annihilation of animal life. Better yet, we can outlaw guns, and thus put a rein on man's instinct for the kill.
>
> Hunting is an odious sport.
>
> Jack Fleishman
> Lansing, Michigan

ASSIGNMENT

Suppose you are moved to react strongly to a news item, a legislative act, a family situation, or a school problem. You might want to make your view known.

How do you do this?

STEP 1: READ YOUR NEWSPAPER CAREFULLY

Determine its position on issues that affect you. See whether you agree or disagree. Suppose, for example, there is an announcement that students will have to take lengthy tests in each subject they are studying in school and you are opposed to taking so many tests.

STEP 2: SET DOWN YOUR POSITION

Your position might be that students are burdened all year with far too many tests.

STEP 3: SUPPORTING REASONS

Reason 1: Taking five subjects and preparing homework in each is enough responsibility

Reason 2: Many of the tests given do not really measure what is learned in class

Reason 3: Testing makes people nervous and anxious

STEP 4: PUT IT TOGETHER EDITORIALLY

Remember, you are writing to a newspaper, not to a friend or to the principal of the school. Therefore, write directly, clearly, but convincingly.

Example

The Highland Monitor
276 Midland Road
Trenton, New Jersey

Dear Editor:

In the April 26 issue of your publication you announced a schoolwide testing program. I wish to make clear all the reasons why I am adamantly opposed to the idea of testing.

First of all, students with four or five major subjects are burdened with enough preparation. As for me, I find the responsibility of doing required readings and completing written assignments to be staggering. In addition, tests rarely prove anything because they do not measure what was taught in class. If there is no relationship between tests and learning, then why be subjected to such torture? Finally, testing is a process that makes students nervous and anxious. Every time I take one I freeze and therefore never do as well as I should.

It is time that the school realized the terrible consequences that tests have when they are given so frequently. Surely there must be a better way of measuring progress than sending young people into rooms and having them write for three hours. I'm all for doing away with them.

Analysis

The basic idea of opposition to tests is powerfully conveyed through references to specific situations that all students can identify with. No matter whether or not the readers agree, they can feel the power of the writer's stand.

This is what a good editorial does: makes an effective statement in a convincing way.

Follow-Up Exercise

Now write your own editorial on one of the following:

1. Old age homes

2. People who commit murder

3. The effect of television

4. Getting along with parents

5. Jobs for teenagers

6. Drug laws

7. Lowering the age for quitting school

Chapter Three

STAGES OF WRITING

Writing begins with an idea but then the writer is faced with developing a composition from that idea. The writer puts impressions and facts into an organized format. Finally, the composition is reworked, reshaped, often rewritten completely. This chapter, then, shows you how to structure your ideas in an effective manner.

HOW DO I WRITE AN OUTLINE?

(Credit: Donato Leo. From Freelance Photographers Guild.)

The photograph shows one kind of outline. How does this outline compare with the one you prepare before you write a composition?

An outline is a simple plan to help the writer put his thoughts in order. You can think of an outline as a reminder of several main ideas that must go into a composition. You can also think of it as a pre-arranged pattern that will guide you in your final writing. It is always strongly recommended that writers think through their topics carefully before writing so that the order and consistency of main ideas is maintained. Writing an outline will enable you to structure just what you want to say.

Example

Plant Robbery

I. Extent of New Crime Wave
   A. Southern states report plant robberies worth $12,000 each week
   B. Stolen plants sold in the north

II. Reasons for Rise in Plant Thefts — Plants Are Booming Business

III. Kinds of Plants Stolen
   A. Dracaena
   B. Ferns
   C. Hanging baskets

IV. Where Plants Are Stolen
   A. Apartment living rooms
   B. Condominium sun decks
   C. Suburban yards

V. How Plant Robbery is Being Fought
   A. Punishment increased
   B. Self-help group
      1. Telephone "hot line"
      2. Private detective hired

HOW DO I WRITE A COMPOSITION FROM AN OUTLINE?

PROBLEM

How do I write a composition from an outline?

Once you've written an outline, your job of writing a composition is more than half done. You now have before you a carefully written guide showing what topics will be in your composition, what will be discussed in each topic, and in what order these topics will appear in your composition.

Solution

STEP 1: MAKE COMPLETE SENTENCES

The obvious way an outline differs from a completed composition is that it is not in full sentences. Instead, phrases are used in an outline to indicate to the writer what ideas will be discussed. Now it's time to turn those phrases into complete sentences.

The most important things to remember when writing a composition from an outline are:

1. You *don't* have to follow your outline *exactly*!

2. You *don't* have to use the same words in your composition that you used in your outline. Remember, since you wrote your outline just as a guide to yourself, you didn't have to be concerned about choosing words that would be interesting and clear to another reader. Wherever you think you can improve on your outline, be sure to do so.

3. Don't think of each line of your outline as a separate sentence. For instance, look at topic III of the outline on Plant Robbery.

   III. Kinds of Plants Stolen
      A. Dracaena
      B. Fern
      C. Hanging Baskets

It would be pretty dull to write: "Three kinds of plants are stolen. Dracaena are stolen. Ferns are stolen. Hanging baskets are stolen."

You can make your composition more interesting by combining several ideas into one sentence. Is this an improvement? "The kinds of plants stolen are dracaena, ferns, and hanging baskets."

That certainly is better, but now watch how a good writer did it! "Dracaena and staghorn fern are the two most commonly stolen plants, but any hanging basket is bait for a quick hit and run."

This sentence has many words in it that are not in the outline. The writer has told us that *staghorn* fern is commonly stolen, which helps make the facts clearer to the reader. Also, he refers to the stealing of a hanging basket as a quick hit and run which, by making the reader think of a car accident, makes the sentence more exciting.

STEP 2: DIVIDE INTO PARAGRAPHS

Your outline will be helpful to you when you have to decide what ideas should go together in paragraphs. First, try to make each major topic a separate paragraph.

For instance, a professional writer might turn one topic in the outline —

V. How Plant Robbery Is Being Fought
    A. Punishment increased
    B. Self-help group
        1. Telephone "hot line"
        2. Private detective hired

— into a paragraph like this:

The crime is so serious that in Florida the punishment for stealing plants has been increased. A self-help association has established a telephone "hot line" for victimized plant owners and has hired its own private detective to try to catch the thieves green-handed.

After making each major topic into a paragraph, examine the paragraphs carefully. If a paragraph seems too long, with too many different ideas in it, you can divide it into two or more paragraphs. On the other hand, if you have several short paragraphs, they can be combined to form one paragraph. For example, the following three major topics have been combined into one paragraph:

II. Reasons for Rise in Plant Thefts — Plants are Booming Business
III. Kinds of Plants Stolen
    A. Dracaena
    B. Fern
    C. Hanging baskets
IV. Where Plants Are Stolen
    A. Apartment living rooms
    B. Condominium sun decks
    C. Suburban yards

Combined paragraph

The explanation for the wave of plant robbery is clear enough: plants are a booming business. "The whole U.S. has gone plant crazy," says a successful plant dealer. Dracaena and staghorn fern are the two most commonly stolen plants, but any hanging basket is bait for a quick hit and run. Plant robbers are now stealing with equal daring from apartment living rooms and condominium sun decks. And in suburbia, they simply move into yards at night and dig the plants out of the ground.

Model Composition

Now compare the outline that we developed with the completed composition written from the outline. First, sentences were formed, then paragraphs were built with those sentences. Because the author had prepared a thoughtful outline, the writing of the composition was not too difficult.

Plant Robbery

A new crime has blossomed in the U.S.: plant robbery. In southern states about $12,000 worth of plants are stolen every week. Almost every night trucks carrying stolen greenery leave secret meeting places in central Florida and head north to make illegal sales.

The explanation for the wave of plant robbery is clear enough: plants are a booming business. "The whole U.S. has gone plant crazy," says a successful plant dealer. Dracaena and staghorn fern are the two most commonly stolen plants, but any hanging basket is bait for a quick hit and run. Plant robbers are now stealing with equal daring from apartment living rooms and condominium sun decks. And in suburbia, they simply move into yards at night and dig the plants out of the ground.

The crime is so serious that in Florida the punishment for stealing plants has been increased. A self-help association has established a telephone "hot line" for victimized plant owners and has hired its own private detective to try to catch the thieves green-handed.

HOW DO I BEGIN A COMPOSITION?

Mom always reveals this quality in the way she acts with us. For example, she listens to me when I have a problem. She has patience to hear me out and not dismiss what is bothering me as silly. Further, when my father comes home from work, she makes an effort to make him feel comfortable and to listen to his day's events. As I think back, I can clearly recall relatives coming to the house to tell Mom matters of family concern, and she would always lend an attentive ear. In so many ways, my mother is a patient, caring person.

How would you begin this portrait of a mother? What opening line would you start with?

What does an introductory sentence have to do with the rest of the writing?

PROBLEM

I don't know how to begin anything.

Neither did Joseph Heller, the famous author, know how to begin. Heller, whose book and moving picture was the triumphant *Catch-22*, took eleven years to finish his second novel.

During a television interview Heller said that a first sentence needed special attention — apparently eleven years' worth! You don't have to spend that long on your introduction to an essay, but writing a beginning does take time and thought; let's face it, a beginning often can be frighteningly difficult to write.

Solution

But, how do I begin?

STEP 1: DECIDE ON A SPECIFIC TOPIC

You begin with a clear idea, an idea that is worth writing about, worth reading about. This idea can usually be expressed in one sentence. Suppose you want to write an essay about the New York Police Department. Fine, but what are you going to tell about the New York Police Department? Its size? How they catch criminals? How the department is organized? How it trains its policemen? The racial and ethnic composition of the force? The weapons used by the policemen? We could go on! In order to begin, you must decide on the one main idea of your essay, an idea specific enough to develop completely in the paper that you want to write.

STEP 2: MAKE A LIST OF POSSIBLE OPENING SENTENCES

Suppose you choose to write on the topic "Women can serve as police officers as well as men." Actually, by deciding on a topic more specific than the New York Police Department you have focused on a good introductory sentence. You are ready to begin. You have many alternatives open to you. Here are some sample beginning sentences — not all good!

1. *Women can serve as police officers as well as men.* This is not a bad beginning. It is simple and direct and expresses the main idea. Since there are some people — especially some men — who might question the truth of this statement, it will probably provoke the reader to go on. How easy it was to get this first sentence! But don't be fooled. Much thinking came before we got this sentence into our heads.

2. *First there was Adam and Eve and we know what happened in the Garden of Eden.* Watch out! This sentence is much too far from the immediate topic, even for a long essay. For a short essay it would be a disaster! It will take the writer too many words to get the reader to the New York Police Department and your reader may have been misled. He may have thought he began a composition about the Bible or love and jealousy or snakes.

3. *Can a woman be as good a police officer as a man?* Here is an example of a variation from the simple opening statement. You probably learned to begin with a question in elementary school. It works! Lots of professional writers start with a question, especially if there is no obvious answer. Notice that the main idea of the essay is automatically expressed in a question beginning.

4. *Police Commissioner Byrne has announced that the New York City Police Department will continue to hire female officers this year.* An important statement by a recognized authority — especially if it leads directly into your main idea — can produce a strong beginning. Statements like this one have to be researched. Look in newspapers, books, and magazines for a beginning for your paper.

5. *Shakespeare may have said that "Women are soft, mild, pitiful and flexible" but today they are being hired as police officers in New York City.* A famous quotation can give lots of excitement to a beginning sentence. Here the quotation did not express the main idea of the essay, but the rest of the sentence bends it smoothly to create a beginning that will make the reader continue reading.

6. *In the last year seven policemen have been saved from death by heroic efforts of policewomen.* When the reader sees a startling fact right at the beginning of an essay, he is tempted to read on. The main idea — although not stated here — is implied and can be cleared up in the next sentence.

7. *The police car screamed around the corner, slammed into the curb and stopped. Revolvers drawn, the two officers jumped out. One was a woman.* One effective introduction is the use of the anecdote or little story. You'll have to follow the anecdote with a clear statement of the main idea, though, and you'll have to avoid the trap of getting so involved in the story that you never get to develop your main idea.

There are two good "rules" to follow when writing any introduction. First, the beginning should tell readers what the entire essay is about, and second, the beginning should give readers this information in an interesting way that will make them want to read on. After all, you are writing the essay for people to read, and if they do not know what they are going to read about, or if they feel they do not want to read what you've written, they will stop reading at the beginning, no matter how spectacular your writing is later on.

You might try this technique; some writers do this all the time when they feel too hung up on a beginning. Write a simple, straightforward beginning (I spent my summer vacation in a factory.) and then plunge into the essay itself. Later you may come back to the first paragraph, and, drawing perhaps on an idea you feel you have worked out well later in the paper, revise the simple introduction or write a new one, making sure it still states the main idea clearly. This would also be a good time to check to see if the beginning was interesting — interesting enough to make sure the reader would want to read on. In this procedure even if you never get back to the first paragraph you still have a simple introduction, and that's better than none at all, and sometimes even better than some fancy beginning. For instance, starting an essay with a joke may capture your audience's attention, but if the joke is not related to the rest of the essay, you are certain to lose the reader's attention.

STEP 3: LIMIT YOUR INTRODUCTION

How long should the introduction be? The shorter the essay, the shorter the beginning. On examinations students are often asked to write essays from 150-740 words in length. A good measure is to use about 10 per cent of your essay for the beginning, but most introductions are better shorter than longer than this. Unless you are involved in a very long paper, one short paragraph — sometimes one sentence — does the whole job.

Follow-Up Exercises

Read the following passage to see whether all the sentences relate to the opening one:

The Beginning of the Day Is Important to Me
When I get up, I am often tired and confused so I do calisthenics and jog a mile. Actually, this routine puts me into shape and prepares me for the day's hectic events. Later, while riding on the bus, I think about yesterday and consider what I have yet to do, and those thirty minutes really put me into the right mood and frame of mind for my studies. When I walk to school . . .

Write a beginning for each of the topics listed below:

1. Behind the scene in sports
2. Motorcycles
3. Are we eating poison?

4. Decorating your own room
5. Styles in shoes

HOW DO I END A COMPOSITION?

Unlike other students, I love going to school. Actually, I look forward to it each day when I rise out of bed. First, I feel stimulated intellectually in the classes I attend. Second, I value the friendships I have made and wish to continue. Third, I participate eagerly in the sports program of my school, which develops my body and keeps me trim.

Why is this paragraph incomplete?

Without an ending any piece of writing is incomplete. Think of a conclusion or ending as the dessert of a meal, the last part that brings the eating experience to a satisfying close. Just as a typical meal consists of an appetizer, a main course, and a dessert, the typical writing pattern is an introduction (the opener or appetizer), a body (the main course), and a conclusion (the dessert).

PROBLEM

I don't know how to end anything.

The illustrating paragraph presents a logical development of an idea (how much the writer likes school) with suporting reasons (intellectual, social, and physical stimulation). But it is not tied all together in any convincing way. In other words, the conclusion is missing.

Solution

Which ending would be the most suitable choice?

1. I really don't know why so many young people dislike school.

2. If you have to go to school, you might as well make the best of it.

3. Attending school, then, helps me to be a well-rounded person.

Do you see which sentence should round out the paragraph?

No. 3 is the only sentence that reemphasizes or restates the writer's initial idea. But note how the writer changes the idea of loving school to the effect it has on him — making him well-rounded. This is an effective and important way of saying something a bit differently.

Other Purposes of a Conclusion

EXAMPLE 1: A CONCLUSION CAN MAKE A PREDICTION OR PROJECT SOME HOPE FOR THE FUTURE.

Note how this writer makes a point, supports it, then makes a prediction as a conclusion.

Euthanasia, known as mercy killing, should be the human right of those incurable patients who are suffering while awaiting inevitable doom. Terminally ill cancer victims kept alive and given morphine or other painkillers are among the living-dead, and should be given a choice to end their lives mercifully. Brain damaged accident victims kept technically alive by machines, since they cannot function on their own beyond a vegetable state, are a burden to both family and state, and should be allowed to die with dignity. Any other person who is told that there is no hope medically or otherwise should also be told that he or she can sign a Living Will, a legal document pledging a desire to end a life that is painful. *Some day, I hope, our society will recognize the need for this human right and allow its individuals the choice to leave this world of suffering with some degree of dignity.*

EXAMPLE 2: CONCLUSIONS CAN ALSO SUM UP OUTSTANDING QUALITIES OF PEOPLE.

The greatest mother in this wide, wide world lives in my house. Always a considerate lady, Mom puts her family first and never complains about work or responsibility. If kindness earned money, my mother would be richer than Croesus, for on no occasion has she ever forgotten anyone's birthday, nor has she ever failed to come to another person's help when she was needed. She is a Niagara of love, giving love but not always receiving it. When you meet my Mom, you will not only feel love but you will actually see it in her eyes and her every gesture. *I don't say every woman has to be like my mother, but if more people showed consideration, kindness, and love, how much better this world would be.*

EXAMPLE 3: CONCLUSIONS CAN ALSO HELP TO BRING AN EXPERIENCE TO A CLEAR DEFINITE ENDING.

In storytelling, for example, we relate an event by giving certain action details, then we conclude by stating the result or the consequence. For example:

The serious auto accident we were in one day shook me up for a long time. We had not seen the speeding motorist when he swooped in from the left, and therefore we had no time to avert a head-on collision. I closed my eyes and prayed for the best. The momentum of the crash felt like an earthquake, and I felt my body being lifted and controlled by some powerful force. The next thing I knew I was lying some ten yards from the hulks of two cars, with flames shooting sky-high, and listening to the moans of the other driver as he lay tangled inside. I tried to lift myself but was seized by pain that ripped through my entire body. Luckily, the police cars and an ambulance came in the nick of time and rescued the driver before the explosion jolted the ground. I was lifted gently from the grass and placed inside the ambulance, tended to by a nurse, and zoomed off to the hospital where a deep gash on my left side was bandaged. Luckily, I had no serious injuries, and so I was released the next day. *Such an experience – the fear, the sudden happening – leaves a psychological scar that never heals. I am always fearful it will happen again.*

As we have seen, conclusions can serve to (1) summarize, (2) restate, (3) emphasize, (4) make a prediction, and (5) state a result. How you end your writing depends on what you put into it, how you develop it, and on which main idea you are building.

Follow-Up Exercise

Read the following passage and write an appropriate conclusion:

Franklin Delano Roosevelt's home in Hyde Park, New York, is a national historic site as well as the preservation of a great man's style of living. One hall is completely filled with photographs and personal letters dating from the man's childhood to maturity. Another part of the house shows his contributions to the world — laws, treaties, social acts, and humanitarian deeds — as well as his role during the Depression and World War II. A third section of this house centers around Eleanor, his wife, and her contributions to social, economic, and humanitarian progress. Her trophies, honors, and awards are conspicuously displayed. If you follow the rooms in order and read the captions carefully, you will gain a clear picture of the Roosevelt family. _____

_____

_____

What conclusion would you write?

HOW DO I DECIDE ON A TITLE?

(Credit: Daniel Nardi. From Freelance Photographers Guild.)

If you had to decide on a title for this picture, what would you write?

1. Disaster in the City

2. FIRE!

3. Decision Under Pressure

4. Fire Fighters

PROBLEM

Study the illustration and the suggested titles. Which of the four would serve as the best choice of a title?

Your choice would depend on (1) what details you see in the scene, and (2) how these details make you feel. Both together constitute a focus from which a title will emerge.

Visual details: Firemen wearing oxygen tanks, smoke pouring from building, a city street, firemen using hoses from ladders

Feelings: Tension, fear, courage, strength, bravery

Solution

If these details give you a strong sense of disaster, then you would select No. 1. If, on the other hand, all these details make you so tense that you might have nightmares, then you would probably select No. 2. Perhaps the details make you think of the courage and valor of fire fighters. In that case, No. 4 would suffice. But, if you view the details of this scene as brave men deciding on the best course of action, then No. 3 would be your choice.

PROBLEM

Read the following passage with the idea of deciding on a title to suit it.

The city of Istanbul, Turkey, rises tall above the blue waters of the Bosphorus. The melodic wail of the call to prayer mixes with the strange sounds of the street. Women, with faces covered, slide through the street; waterboys spill out a penny's worth of cold liquid; fishermen hold up giantsize catches wrapped in newspapers; ragged-looking urchins skip and hop in the puddles of the street. Ships of all nations ply their way through the water, flying their flags proudly. Gulls, sweeping down on the minarets of the mosques, call loudly. The smells of food sold openly meet the nostrils with delight and flavor. The setting sun casts a gray shadow in the courtyards of wooden frame homes that look as if they have been there forever. It is, this Istanbul, a city that dances even on one's mind and imagination.

What title would you give it?

Solution

STEP 1: SELECT THE PROMINENT DETAILS

1. Blue waters
2. Call to prayer

3. Sounds of the street
4. Women with covered faces

5. Water boys spilling out water
6. Fishermen selling fish
7. Youngsters playing about
8. Ships sailing by

9. Gulls making sounds
10. The smell of food
11. The setting sun

STEP 2: DERIVE A FEELING

All these details, as one total view of a city, convey a feeling or a mood. They help to create an atmosphere that is characteristic of Istanbul — an atmosphere unlike that of any other city. Reading this description, then, should give you the feeling of:

1. Excitement
2. Exotic flavor
3. Uniqueness
4. Being alive
5. Desire to be there
6. Dreaming

STEP 3: APPLY A SUITABLE TITLE

The title you use, then, should reflect the special details and the feeling you get from them. If you decide that a proper title should be "An Interesting City," you would not be capturing the essence. After all, a lot of cities are interesting for many reasons, but how many have Istanbul's matchless look? But if you concluded that an appropriate title should be "Istanbul: An Exotically Different Place," you would not only be capturing a focus, but stimulating readers to want to know more.

All good titles are so appealing that practically anyone would be eager to read to learn more. In this case, the reader would naturally wish to discover in what ways Istanbul is exotic and exciting. The details of this piece would then satisfy this desire.

Follow-Up Exercise

Now you are on your own. Apply a title that best fits the following passage:

I felt his hand in my pocket and jerked forward. When I reached over to stop the stranger from taking my wallet, he jumped from the seat and ran from the train. Surprisingly, I leaped from the train and raced after him. By the time I reached the exit door, the fleeting figure was too far ahead for me to catch him. In frustration, I yelled, "Stop that man! He tried to steal my wallet!" But no one heard for the street was empty and deserted. As I reached into my pocket to reassure myself that the wallet was still there, I breathed a sigh of relief.

HOW DO I DEVELOP A PIECE OF WRITING FROM A TITLE ITSELF?

ASSIGNMENT

Write a fully developed, organized paragraph, using one of the following titles:

A Moment of Happiness

My Personal Dream

A Person Dear to Me

A Gift of Love

A Television Program I Would Never Miss

Solution

STEP 1: MAKE A SELECTION

Let's say you are drawn to the third one, "A Person Dear to Me," because there is indeed someone whom you love and respect. Perhaps it is a friend you are especially fond of.

STEP 2: OUTLINE DETAILS

Let us take that friend and list his traits that endear him or her to you.

1. He always listens to my problems.

2. He is always kind and considerate.

3. He always comes through when I am troubled.

STEP 3: SUPPORT DETAILS WITH EXAMPLES

You must now think of specific ways your friend shows these traits of listening, being kind and considerate, and coming through for you. Therefore, revise your outline.

1. He always listens to my problems.
   Once, when I was about to leave home, he talked me into staying.

2. He is always kind and considerate.
   When I won a fencing award, he celebrated by surprising me with a party.

3. He always comes through when I am in trouble.
   When my father died, he stayed with me for a few days.

STEP 4: DECIDE ON THE CENTRAL FEELING

Now decide what kind of feeling you have knowing there is a friend who will always listen, always be kind and considerate, and who will always come through in times of trouble.

  If gratitude is what you feel, then make that the main feeling to come out of your writing.

STEP 5: GEAR EVERYTHING TO THE TITLE

Look back at your title, "A Person Dear to Me," and make sure everything you write relates to that.

STEP 6: PUT IT ALL TOGETHER

You have all you need to complete a good piece of writing. But be sure to construct sentences that are lively, complex and interesting.

STEP 7: THE POLISHED JOB

A Person Dear to Me

  Jerry Ornstein, a friend of mine for many years, is someone I admire greatly. To begin with, he always manages to listen to my problems when I need help. For example, once when I tried to leave home because of a problem with my family, Jerry sat down to talk with me and to make clear that staying and dealing with the problem was a better solution than running away. On every occasion I can think of, Jerry has been kind and considerate. When I won a fencing award, he secretly planned a surprise party and invited all my friends. I was so delighted that I cried. A third reason why I admire this boy is that he always comes through when I am in trouble. Last year, when my father died, and I was feeling so sad, Jerry came to my house to stay with me for a few days. Actually, his presence at that time made me adjust better to the tragedy. When I look back on our relationship, I see Jerry Ornstein as more than a friend — he is a priestly person.

Evaluation

If you examine this paragraph, you will note we have included all the details about Jerry's character. Also, the feeling that comes out of it is one of admiration. More important, though, is that the entire writing follows from the title, "A Person Dear to Me."

HOW DO I PROOFREAD WHAT I WRITE?

Proofreading is merely taking the time to look over your writing to be sure it is neat, correct, and presentable. It is, really, an excellent technique. The opposite is true: not reviewing your writing at the end is a sloppy technique that may result in poorer quality and therefore a lower mark. It boils down to one skill, and that is the ability to reread everything you write to check out the following:

1. Organization

2. Order

3. Unity and coherence

4. Grammar and syntax

5. Punctuation

6. Spelling and usage

7. Neatness and clarity

8. Completeness and thoroughness

9. Sentence variety

10. Paragraphing

PROBLEM

How do you proofread these areas?

Solution

STEP 1: ORGANIZATION – HOW THE SEQUENCE OF EVENTS OR DETAILS IS PUT TOGETHER

For example, you may find that in writing a paper discussing high school sports you may have strayed into college or neighborhood sports. That would mean you didn't organize tightly around the topic area.

STEP 2: ORDER – HOW YOU ARRANGE OR PLACE THESE IDEAS

For example, if you are describing a wedding, you would be expected to start at the moment you arrived for the ceremony and follow through with the reception, in that order, because they are chronological. Otherwise your description of the event may be confusing.

STEP 3: UNITY AND COHERENCE – HOW YOU TIE IN ALL YOUR DETAILS TO THE GENERAL AREA

In other words, if your purpose in writing is to tell about a mystery program on television, you would be expected to include as many facts about the show itself and not talk about other kinds of programs. The way to judge this is to reread your topic idea and ask: "Do all my facts and details unite to develop this one idea?"

STEP 4: GRAMMAR AND SYNTAX – ALL GOOD WRITING DEMANDS GRAMMATICAL PRECISION.

Syntax is the correctness with which you express yourself according to writing standards. Here are some common errors to avoid:

1. One of my books were stolen.

   Correction: One of my books *was* stolen.

2. In the book it says the people were poor.

   Correction: The book states the people were poor.

3. Anyone would recognize their own house.

   Correction: Anyone would recognize *his* own house.

4. He loves chess, tennis, and to play football.

   Correction: He loves chess, tennis, *and football.*

5. He bought a dresser from a man weighing 400 pounds.

   Correction: He bought a dresser, weighing 400 pounds, from a man.

STEP 5: PUNCTUATION – PLACING COMMAS, QUOTATION MARKS, APOSTROPHES, COLONS, AND SEMICOLONS WHERE THEY BELONG

Using these punctuation marks correctly can make the difference between clarity and confusion.

1. John who is my best friend moved away to a nicer bigger neighborhood.

   Correction: John, who is my best friend, moved away to a nicer, bigger neighborhood.

2. Jerrys car is newer than Franks.

   Correction: Jerry's car is newer than Frank's.

3. When I asked him where the theater was he said if you turn right you'll see the Rivoli.

   Correction: When I asked him where the theater was, he said, "If you turn right you'll see the Rivoli."

4. School is very demanding, you have to work hard.

   Correction: School is very demanding; you have to work hard.

5. I have a lot of things to do on my day off, clean, wash, shop, and run errands.

  Correction: I have a lot of things to do on my day off: clean, wash, shop, and run errands.

STEP 6: SPELLING AND USAGE

If you are a weak speller, there is no magical cure — you must rely on a dictionary. After you complete any essay, always take the time to check spellings. But with regard to usage, be careful of some pairs of words, such as:

1. (affect, effect)
   The cold *affects* me terribly.
   The cold has a terrible *effect* on my legs.

2. (all together, altogether)
   We were standing *all together*.
   Altogether there are too many people here.

3. (principle, principal)
   Which *principle* do you live by?
   What is your *principal* reason for leaving home?

STEP 7: NEATNESS AND CLARITY

If your handwriting is illegible, the best thing to do is print or type the whole paper. A sloppily handwritten paper may lead to a failing mark.

STEP 8: COMPLETENESS AND THOROUGHNESS – DEVELOPING FULLY ALL YOUR IDEAS

You must give details and explanations, and write a conclusion at the end. This also refers to expanding on a topic and telling all you know.

STEP 9: SENTENCE VARIETY – USING SENTENCES THAT CREATE INTEREST AND NOT DULLNESS

For example:

My father is a busy man. He works long hours. He has little time for his family.
Correction: My father is a busy man — he works long hours and has little time for his family.

STEP 10: PARAGRAPHING – DEVELOPING ONE IDEA FULLY BEFORE GOING ON TO THE NEXT

> I love to play tennis outdoors. Somehow, maybe because of the sun and the cool air, my game is always superior. Besides, there's something about an open court that stimulates my skill and movement. Clay courts especially are advantageous because my feet dig in better. This is not so for squash, a sport

that requires an indoor area. Since squash is played on a smaller court, there is no real advantage to playing outdoors. Anyway, I seem to do better in squash indoors than I do in tennis outdoors.

If you read this writing for the ideas alone, you will note that the first part deals with the writer's love of tennis, which is developed through "my feet dig better." The second part (new paragraph) starts with "This is not so for squash," which leads into a different sport.

Every time you leave an idea and start another, you must begin with a new paragraph.

ASSIGNMENT

This section has dealt with ten areas of writing that require proofreading after the writing is done. To give you a better idea of how important this step is, try to proofread the following passage to determine the variety of errors that should be corrected.

The more I think about Arkansas and its affect on me, the more I miss it and the people. Especially my grandparents. I recollect a lot about my boyhood years. The friends I had were very close, and even when I was younger one of them took their boats to take me on a cruise across the lake. I remember his saying I really want to be your friend. My grandmother and my grandfather both were hardworking people, and they recommended I become a farmer like the generation before me. We lived altogether in a one-family stone ranch. I can remember throwing stones into the neighborhood creek. My friends did also. Because of it, we were often late getting home. My parents reaction though was one of anger, because they expected me to be grown up and responsible long before my time. Life in this coastal town in California was slow but comfortable, and I miss it.

Solution

Now note what good proofreading can accomplish:

The more I think about Arkansas and its *effect* on me, the more I miss it and the people, especially my grandparents, who were hardworking people who recommended I become a farmer like the generation before me. *But, of course, I was too young to pay heed to such advice.*

I recollect a lot about my boyhood there. The friends I had were very close and even when I was younger, one of them took *his boat* to take me on a cruise across the lake. I remember his saying, *"I really want to be your friend."*

We lived together in a one-family stone ranch, from which I can remember throwing stones into the neighborhood creek. My friends did also, and because of it, we were often late getting home. My parents' reaction, though, was one of anger, because they expected me to be grown up and responsible long before my time.

    Life in this coastal town in California was slow but comfortable, and I miss it.

Evaluation

Note the many changes in the writing above. Many errors have been corrected. Sometimes, symbols in the margin will remind you of the kind of error and what must be done. Symbols to show errors are very important because English teachers use them. Therefore, you should become familiar with them. They also provide a guide to self-improvement.

Common symbols:

WW   Wrong word

SS   Sentence structure

SV   Sentence variety

P   Punctuation

¶   Begin a new paragraph

Agr   Pronoun or verb does not agree with the antecedent.

Gr   Error in grammar or syntax

SF   Sentence fragment

RS   Run-on sentence

Org   Ideas not organized well

Cl   Meaning is not clear (clarity needed)

Voc   Wrong choice of word (vocabulary)

Id   Wrong idiom

?   What do you mean?

Awk   Awkward writing

T   Wrong verb tense

    Proofreading, though it's the last step, is just as important as the first step in writing. It is not only a way of showing that you are careful but a means of eliminating unnecessary errors that your teacher will pick up. The important questions to ask are:

1. Is my composition divided into well-organized paragraphs?

2. Did I stick to the topic idea and develop all my points?

3. Are my sentences well-structured and do they have variety?

4. Are the words I used the very best choice?

5. Did I check all my spellings?

    Never, never write anything without taking the time to read it over to find your own faults.

Chapter Four

SPECIAL SKILLS THAT DEVELOP STYLE AND CLARITY

Previous chapters have considered ways of generating ideas, thinking them through, outlining them, and organizing them. Chapter Four emphasizes the skills required to present these ideas effectively.

The following sections show you how to punctuate, how to select the correct words, how to use dialogue, and how to make your writing fresh and vital. Knowing these skills, along with the rules of standard usage, will lead to more convincing communication.

HOW CAN COMMAS HELP MY WRITING?

> **PROBLEM**
>
> I don't know when to use commas, or even how they can help my writing.

The comma is a very useful tool in making your meaning clearer. If you use it correctly, your writing will be more effective, and the reader will find it easier to understand what you have to say. Like any other tool, the comma is as good as you know how to use it.

How, then, do you use it?

Solution

Read the following passage and try to determine where you would place commas.

My house which is located on a dead-end street has a marvelous beautiful view. Really it is the kind of house that many people dream of owning and I wouldn't trade it for any other. In addition when I think about where I live I feel so grateful. At other times I take my house for granted like an old toy and I may even overlook its value. Though others may think their homes are outstanding I see mine as my castle. Should anyone wish to share the joy of my residence my address is 241 Sexton Street Trenton New Jersey 07985.

Have you placed the commas correctly? If you did, you used a total of 14. Let's see how that works out.

My house, which is located on a dead-end street, has a marvelous, beautiful view. Really, it is the kind of house that many dream of owning, and I wouldn't trade it for any other. In addition, when I think about where I live, I feel so grateful. At other times, I take it for granted, like an old toy, and overlook its value. Though others may think their homes are outstanding, I see mine as my castle. Should anyone wish to share the joy of my residence, my address is 241 Sexton Street, Trenton, New Jersey 07985.

REASON 1: CERTAIN CLAUSES THAT CAN BE OMITTED WITHOUT CHANGING THE MEANING OF A SENTENCE RECEIVE COMMAS.

Example: My house, which is located on a dead-end street, has a marvelous, beautiful view.

If you omitted the clause "which is located on a dead-end street," you would be left with "My house has a marvelous, beautiful view." That is the basic sentence and by removing the clause the basic meaning has not been changed.

REASON 2: *PARENTHETICAL (UNNECESSARY) WORDS OR WORDS OF EMPHASIS MAY BE SEPARATED.*

Independent clauses may be separated by placing the commas before the conjunction.

Example: Really, it is the kind of house that many dream of owning, and I wouldn't trade it for any other.

REASON 3: *TRANSITIONAL EXPRESSIONS (JOINING WORDS) MAY BE SEPARATED.*

Introductory adverbial clauses should be separated from the main clauses.

Example: In addition, when I think about where I live, I feel so grateful.

REASON 4: *REFERENCES OR FIGURES OF SPEECH MAY BE SET OFF BY COMMAS.*

Example: At other times, I take it for granted, like an old toy, and overlook its value.

"Like an old toy" is not necessary to the sentence. It is added merely to emphasize the point of taking the house for granted. Commas are placed, therefore, to show that these words are not essential to the basic idea.

REASON 5: *FULL ADDRESSES ARE SET OFF WITH COMMAS TO SEPARATE THE STREET FROM THE CITY, THE CITY FROM THE STATE, BUT NOT THE STATE FROM THE ZIP CODE.*

Example: I live at 24 East Boynton Road, Scarsdale, New York 11796.

Review of Reasons for Setting Off Words with Commas

1. Dependent clauses are separated from independent clauses.
2. Parenthetical expressions are set off.
3. Transitional words are separated.
4. Figures of speech may be omitted.
5. Full addresses are set off with commas.

Exercise

Using these five principles, place commas in the proper places in the following paragraph:

> Honestly speaking money is great to have. When you think about it money brings a lot of joy and happiness. Possessing it like owning a rare gem is

power. If I had enough money I would buy the Sheraton Hotel which is located at Seventh Avenue and 56 Street New York New York 10016. It would be something special it really would to have that opportunity.

Other Uses of the Comma

The comma as a punctuation mark has very specific uses. It really is a logical device to make your meaning much clearer to the reader. Note the following situations in which it is used.

Example 1: To avoid confusion

1. I ran back for the ferocious dog was barking.
2. Before swinging Frank held the bat tightly.
3. To fly a plane must have enough fuel.
4. In order to putt Jim had to place the ball on the tee.
5. Outside the yard was clean.

Do you see the problems in clarity above?

Corrections

1. I ran back, for the ferocious dog was barking.
2. Before swinging, Frank held the bat tightly.
3. To fly, a plane must have enough fuel.
4. In order to putt, Jim had to place the ball on the tee.
5. Outside, the yard was clean.

Using the comma correctly in these sentences prevents one idea from running into another.

Example 2: To separate a series of items or things

We went to the country this summer to swim, to hike, to camp out, and to relax.

Example 3: To separate a number of adjectives that describe the same noun.

The brilliant, starry, black sky was beautiful.

Example 4: To separate nonrestrictive clauses or phrases.

The committee, appointed last year, met for the tenth time to discuss the issue.

Certain clauses and phrases are restrictive, which means they cannot be set off by commas.

The one who is the first to enter will get the prize.

The person being called for the first time will have the privilege of speaking.

Example 5: To separate introductory phrases and clauses

In the early morning, I went out to feed the birds.

When you take out the garbage, be sure to wash out the cans.

Example 6: To separate direct address: When you address the person and use a name, you set off the name with commas.

Joe, please come over to help.

Please, Joe, come over to help.

Please come over to help, Joe.

Follow-Up Exercise

Review all the situations that require the use of commas. When you feel you have mastered these principles, use commas in the following passage:

Back in the wilderness of Africa he journeyed from one poor village to another where he saw so many impoverished terrible homes. When he arrived in the region of Angola which is near the border of Zambia he searched for his family. He tried very honestly to make contact with the natives but they avoided him as if he were a plague. To help some people from the local missionary came forth to lend a hand saying they would travel to his family. Upon hearing this he was grateful. The incident that made him happiest was actually finding with the help of others his relatives.

HOW DO I ENRICH MY VOCABULARY IN WRITING?

My teacher is a *real cool guy*. He's good to me and I think he's *nice*.

How can you enrich this vocabulary?

PROBLEM

How do I enrich my vocabulary in writing?

Vocabulary, here, refers to the words you use in writing. Sometimes the choice of a word determines how well the reader will be able to understand your ideas. If the word is too common, too general, or inappropriate, then the effect of the writing will be poor.

Example

    Mount Washington is a big mountain. It is way up in the hills of Vermont. If you go up to the top, you can look out and see a long way. It is the kind of place that people like because it is away from the cities. The weather is nice there, the scenery beautiful, and the view good.

  The trouble with this paragraph is that the words this writer used do not convey the flavor of what it is like to be in this special place. Words like *big, way up, go up, look out, a long way, away, nice,* and *good* are very limited. These words are not specific enough to help the reader visualize the scene.

Solution

    Mount Washington is a huge mountain *high up* in the hills of Vermont. If you *ascend* to the top, you can *observe* the scenery below *that stretches beyond sight*. It is the kind of *attraction* that *travelers enjoy* because it is *pleasantly removed* from the cities. The weather is *refreshing* there, the scenery beautiful, and the view *breathtaking*.

Analysis

The trick here in enriching the vocabulary was to remove the common words and substitute more sophisticated ones, those that help the reader visualize the event more clearly.

PROBLEM

How do you know which words to substitute?

In our language there are many idioms and colloquialisms that may be acceptable in speaking but not in writing. Writing demands precision — the exact word in the right place.

EXAMPLE 1: COLLOQUIALISMS

1. My father is a cool guy.

2. That show was outrageous.

3. That show turned me on to stamp collecting.

EXAMPLE 2: PRECISION IN WRITING

1. My father is a *controlled but observant man*.

2. That show was *so funny I laughed throughout*.

3. The show *stimulated me* to collect stamps.

EXAMPLE 3: THE USE OF PRECISE WORDS

New York City's Main Attractions

New York City is a place of history and *tradition*. Every year thousands of visitors *flock* to this busy center. They visit such *sites* as the Empire State Building, the United Nations, and the Statue of Liberty.

The Statue of Liberty, a *structure* that stands for liberty and justice, is a *symbol* for immigrants who come to live here. A gift from France, this *majestic* statue has become a *landmark* for all to see. Now, the U.S. government has *designated* this attraction as part of our national *heritage*. Nothing *signifies* the hope of *downtrodden* people more than this lady with the torch.

Note how the italicized words give the passage not only meaning but importance. Each one of the words has been selected to convey a particular meaning that reinforces the main idea of the passage.

EXAMPLE 4: THE USE OF DRAMATIC WORDS

It was an early morning in winter. The air was *dank*. Above the *pinnacle* of the mountains, you could see the rays of the sun as they struggled to get through the *shrouding* clouds. Morning on a winter day is a *spectacle* I love to witness since I feel so *elated* when I am close to nature. Winter days may be stormy but they do *transport* me to calmness and peace of mind.

Note how the use of words like *dank* and *shrouding* give the reader a sense of gloom, while words like *elated* and *transported* contrast so neatly for their meanings of joy and happiness.

PROBLEM

How do I make the choice?

The right choice of word (known as diction) is the key to effective expression in whatever you write. Dig deeply into your reservoir of vocabulary words for the choice that captures the essence of what you are saying.

Sometimes you have to pin down the specific type of category. The sentences below illustrate vague usage:

1. I hate soup.

2. I just love to smell a flower.

3. I felt such emotion when I met him.

4. I've had this car for five years.

Solution

STEP 1: PIN IT DOWN

1. I hate *lentil soup* especially.

2. I just love to smell a *rose*.

3. I felt such *warmth* when I met him.

4. I've had this *Chrysler* for five years.

STEP 2: SELECT WORDS THAT APPEAL TO THE SENSES

1. The orange moon lay suspended in the sky. (visual)

2. The jet zipped explosively overhead. (auditory)

3. I felt the sting of the sharp spines. (tactile)

4. The meat dish had a heavy, musty odor. (olfactory)

5. Whisky burns as it goes down my throat. (gustatory)

   The right word can determine whether or not a reader sees, feels, tastes, hears, or smells a description you are conveying.

Examples

The train was noisy.

The passengers rode the cars.

The food had a nice smell.

I like the taste of lobster.

It's nice to touch the earth.

Solutions

The train noisily clanged past.

The drowsy-looking passengers rode wearily in the cars.

The food smelled like expensive perfume.

I like the sweet, tender taste of lobster.

It's so exhilarating to touch the soft, crumbly earth.

Follow-Up Exercise

Read the following sentences carefully with an eye to substituting more precise words. Try to use words that are exact as well as sensory.

1. It always feels so cold in winter.

2. Eating sometimes makes me so sick.

3. Hard-rock music just turns me off.

4. My cat always goes crazy when she sees milk.

5. We had a really good time eating out.

WHY IS USAGE SO IMPORTANT?

(Credit: Wide World Photos.)

What is the (principal, principle) feature of the picture?
This is an unusual (cite, site, sight).
What (coarse, course) will traffic take?
Which way will you (turn, tern)?

PROBLEM

I sometimes find I am using the wrong word.

In our language we have many pairs of words that sound alike but are spelled differently. Not knowing the differences in their meaning and use will lead to confusion. For example, look at the following passage to determine the usage errors.

My principle is located in a very pleasant sight in the school. I have all ready visited him many times. Were always friendly together. Its really to bad he can't get around all together. He himself doesn't think its alright, and he seems deeply effected by it. Who's fault is it, I wonder, if the students don't get to see the principle?

Did you notice how many words are used wrongly here? Because they are, the meaning gets lost and the reader is confused.

My *principal* is located in a very pleasant *site* in the school. I have *already* visited him many times. *We're* always friendly together. *It's* really *too* bad he can't get around *altogether*. He himself doesn't think *it's all right*, and he seems deeply *affected* by it. *Whose* fault is it, I wonder, if the students don't get to see the *principal*?

Solution

Let's analyze these and other usage choices for meaning and use so that in the future you need not confuse them.

1. Principal: the main or chief reason; also the head of a school

   Principle: an idea or belief that one holds

   Examples: My *principal* reason for going to college is to be a lawyer.
   Mr. Joe Weathers is the *principal* in our school.
   He held to his *principles* despite the criticism.

2. Site: a particular place or location

   Sight: what you see; an observation you make

   Cite: to mention or to honor

   Examples: The *site* of the last world's fair was Montreal.
   The Grand Canyon is a beautiful *sight*.
   I *sighted* three falcons today.
   Cite three causes of the world war.
   The policeman was *cited* for heroism.

3. Already: previously or before another action

   All ready: prepared to do something

   Examples: When I arrived, he was *already* there.
   We were *all ready* to go on a hike.

4. We're: contraction for "we are"

   Were: from the verb to be

   Where: referring to a place or location

Examples: *Were* you the winner of the lottery?
We're the ones who won the lottery.
Where is the lottery winner?

5. Its: a possessive pronoun showing ownership
   It's: contraction for "it is"
   Examples: The bird watched *its* young.
   It's interesting how some birds watch their young.

6. Altogether: completely or entirely
   All together: a group in the same place for a reason
   Examples: I believe you are *altogether* wrong.
   I believe we should be *all together* on this issue.

7. All right: permissible or right
   Alright: not acceptable in American English
   Examples: I feel *all right*.
   Is it *all right* to stay out late at night?

8. Affect: to change or influence, to produce an effect on
   Effect: the result or consequence; as a verb; to bring about
   Examples: How does the head *affect* you?
   What is the *effect* of the heat on you?

9. Who's: contraction of "who is"
   Whose: a possessive pronoun showing ownership
   Examples: *Who's* the smartest one in your class?
   Whose class has the smartest student?

10. Accept: to take or receive
    Except: excluding or without
    Examples: I gladly *accept* your gift.
    I will take no gift *except* from you.

11. Amount: a sum or total
    Number: units that can be counted
    Examples: The *amount* of money I need is $500.
    The *number* of students in the class is 30.

12. Bring: a movement toward the speaker
    Take: a movement away from the speaker
    Examples: *Bring* me a glass of water.
    Take the glass away.

13. Conscience: concept of right and wrong
    Conscious: aware or awake
    Conscientious: careful; influenced by conscience

Examples: My *conscience* bothered me when I cheated.
                 Are you *conscious* of the importance of the law?
                 He was *conscious* throughout the operation.
                 John is a *conscientious* student.

14. Continual: an interrupted action
    Continuous: an uninterrupted action
    Examples: My dog *continually* demands my attention.
                  The phone rang *continuously* for an hour.

15. Disinterested: without a point of view, unbiased
    Uninterested: not interested
    Examples: When it comes to politics, I am *disinterested*.
                     I am totally *uninterested* in politics.

16. Farther: referring to physical distance
    Further: referring either to distance or to addition
    Examples: The hotel is one mile *farther*.
                We read *further* in the book.
                Further evidence will help us decide.

17. Few: the actual number
    Less: a quantity or degree of
    Examples: There are *few* smokers in the building.
                Smoking has become *less* of a problem.

18. Formally: exactly, traditionally
    Formerly: at one time, before
    Examples: I was *formally* dressed for the wedding.
                Formerly, he was ambassador to England.

19. Healthy: in sound physical shape
    Healthful: promoting health
    Examples: When I eat properly, I am *healthy*.
                Proper food is *healthful*.

20. Hung: an object suspended
    Hanged: a person executed
    Examples: The picture was *hung* above the window.
                The prisoner was *hanged* at dawn.

21. Leave: to place in a spot
    Let: to allow or permit
    Examples: *Leave* the wash on the table.
                Let me take the wash from the table.

22. Lie: to rest or sleep
    Lay: to put or place

Examples: *Lie* down to sleep for awhile.
       Lay the books on the table.

23. Loan: used as a noun

    Lend: to allow someone to borrow

    Examples: I took a *loan* from the bank.
           The bank will *lend* me some money.

24. Personal: private

    Personnel: a staff of workers

    Examples: My marriage is a *personal* matter.
           I reported to the *personnel* office.

25. Stationary: not moving, in one place

    Stationery: referring to writing material

    Examples: Placing the trailer on the cement foundation made it *stationary*.
           I bought a notebook in the *stationery* store.

26. Avocation: a hobby or pastime

    Vocation: a career or professional area

    Examples: Stamp collecting is my chief *avocation*.
           Your choice of *vocation* depends on your skills and interest.

Follow-Up Exercises

1. (Farther, Further) _____ on you will see the lake.

2. (Formerly, Formally) _____ I used to live in Detroit.

3. (conscious, conscientious, conscience) Always act according to your _____.

4. (lie, lay) If you _____ your books on the ground, I'll pick them up.

5. (disinterested, uninterested) Jurors are supposed to be _____ members of a panel.

6. (healthy, healthful) Cigarette smoking is certainly not a _____ thing to do.

7. (amount, number) The _____ of books I have is countless.

8. (principal, principle) Honesty is a _____ I believe in.

9. (effect, affect) Nobody realized the full _____ of pollution.

HOW DO I AVOID CLICHES?

> **PROBLEM**
>
> Whenever I have to write I find I am using ordinary words and expressions. My writing resembles my speaking. My English teacher tells me to be more original, not to use what I hear all the time. His frequent comment is, "Don't use cliches." How do I do this?

Cliches are expressions that have been used so many times they have lost their power. Our language is filled with them and often it is hard to avoid using them. While it may be more acceptable to use them in speaking, in writing they really should be avoided. To use a cliche in writing is to lessen the meaning and impact of what we are saying; most important, cliches keep our writing from sounding like ourselves — we begin to sound like everyone else.

Common Cliches in our Language:

I smell a rat
Knowledge is power
Happy as a lark
Charity begins at home
Beggars can't be choosers
A needle in a haystack
Hard as nails
Strong as a bull
The land of milk and honey

Solution

To avoid cliches:

1. Be inventive.
2. Think of an original way of expressing your idea.

Example

It may be common to say, "I'm so hungry I could eat a cow," but it's not very original. If the idea is to express an insatiable hunger or a desire to eat that is uncontrollable, perhaps a simple alternative would be, "My hunger is so great I could devour a Chicago stockyard."

We all know what is meant by "I'm as fat as a pig," but how many have used "I am so huge I could outmaneuver a battleship?"

The point is that you can take any commonplace situation and make it fresh and new, instead of relying on the unimaginative patterns called cliches. It is a matter of being conscious of the old and outdated and being attuned to the new and challenging. In other words, avoid lazy thinking and lazy communication. Keep your mind alert to the beauty of language and how it can serve you in novel ways. Instead of saying "I am fat as a pig" (cliche), say, "I feel very fat" (simple).

ASSIGNMENT

Here is a student's paper that has been judged as full of cliches by the teacher. Can you identify them?

My Summer Vacation: A Blast

Last summer was a winner of a vacation. I was wild with joy when I learned my family was making plans to sail on a ship to Europe. Paris, a lover's paradise, was our destination of destinations. I would be free as a bird for two whole months! No longer would I be locked in a cage like a monkey. So we headed forth, happy as larks. The waves of the ocean were like giants and the gulls swept down on deck like bombs. When we finally reached Paris, after being sick as dogs, we hurried to our hotel, which was as tall as a skyscraper and as big as a cavern. Never will I forget the bundle of fun I had as a happy tourist in Paris.

Evaluation

Though we can sense the joy of the writer's adventure, the way he uses language loses the effect. It is filled with endless cliches that could be avoided: a winner of a vacation, wild with joy, sail on a ship, a lover's paradise, destination of destinations, as free as a bird, locked in a cage like a monkey, happy as larks, swept down on deck like bombs, sick as dogs, tall as a skyscraper, big as a cavern, bundle of fun, a happy tourist.

Far too many overused and familiar expressions fill this paper. The result is dullness and monotony.

Solution

The best way to improve this piece of writing is to convert each cliche to an expression that is simple and clear.

My Summer Vacation: One to Remember

Last summer *was the most unusual summer I ever had. I was happy* when I learned my family was making plans *to visit Europe.* The city of Paris was our *highlight. I would be free* for two whole months, and no longer would *I have to follow a school schedule.* So we sailed on a modern ocean liner, and *we were all so excited.* The ocean waves were *towering* and *the gulls followed us noisily across the water.* When we finally reached Paris, after *a bout with sea-sickness,* we hurried to our palatial hotel, known for its old-world flavor. Never will I forget the unpredictable joy I had as a tourist in Paris. This was a matchless summer.

The straight, uncluttered prose used here makes the account more acceptable.

Follow-Up Exercises

How would you improve these sentences?

1. My father is a *rock of strength*.

2. My brother is *as slow as a snail*.

3. America is *the land of the free*.

4. *A stitch in time saves nine*.

5. School *turns me off*.

6. You have to *plug away* to make it in any field.

7. This is a country where *you can make it*.

8. I *see stars* every time I am in love.

9. *The heavens lighted up* when I won the contest.

10. Hollywood is *the glamor capital* of the world.

Review

1. Cliches are tiresome, overworked expressions that have lost their effect.

2. If an expression has been used often, avoid it.

3. Think of an original way of conveying an idea or image; often a single statement will do.

4. Don't borrow anyone else's way of saying something.

5. Fresh expressions help to enliven your total writing.

HOW DO I USE IMAGERY IN MY WRITING?

(Credit: Paul Popper. From Freelance Photographers Guild.)

What are the striking aspects of this picture?
How would you describe them?

PROBLEM

How Do I Use Imagery in My Writing?

An image is a word-picture. It is used to create a sense impression. Our language like a painter's brush or a sculptor's tool, can be used to paint or shape very beautiful pictures. Words put together in clever ways can create very effective images. In other words, using imagery in your writing helps to make an object, person, or idea you are describing vivid, colorful, original and fresh. Actually, an image can help readers to visualize a scene in a way they never imagined before.

In speaking, we use imagery all the time. The phrase "He eats like a garbage pickup" gives us a very good idea of the amount this person can consume, much better than does "He eats like a pig." "My father is a tornado when he's set off" reveals the severity of his anger when he's confronted. Even referring to a boy's popularity with girls as "He collects girl friends as a beachcomber gathers shells" is much more concrete than "He's a great lover."

Examples

The woods were like Persian rugs where Autumn was commencing.
The tracks of field mice were stitched across the snow.
Mozart's music can bring your heart to your shoulders.
The singer's phrases ran beautifully together like foothills.
The starving survivors of the shipwreck lifted their match-stick arms.
My father has the heart of an elephant and the mind of a genius.
He sank his teeth into the throat of the book.
As we sailed away, the harbor dwarfed to Japanese-garden proportions.

These and many more phrases are very common in our references to certain people and situations. Though many have been used over and over, and thus have become flat, they can be most effective in speaking. In writing, though, we must be careful not to use cliches (overused images) but rather to devise fresh expressions that capture a scene in a way that was never used before. The more original word-pictures you use, the more striking your writing will be, and the greater its effect will be on the reader. The following is an example of writing with ineffective imagery:

> The path lighted by the moon led me to the house which was buried deeply in the woods. The darkness closed in on me and covered me, and I felt cold and frightened. I didn't really want to go there, but I approached the house and entered a huge room where lights burned brightly. No sooner did I adjust my vision than a voice, loud and clear, made me jump to attention. In this atmosphere of fear, I found I was not too brave, but rather cowardly.

Evaluation

This paragraph describing a night of fear is not very interesting or appealing. The reason for this is that the writer does not make us feel the intensity of night, with its dark and cold elements, nor the scariness of entering an eerie house. What is missing is concrete imagery. The following is the same paragraph written with word-images:

> The moonlit path led me to the house, which was buried *like a squirrel's nut*. The darkness covered me like a shroud, and I felt like a *frozen shank of meat*, fluttery like *an aware bird*. Timidly, I approached the house and entered a massive, broad-beamed room where lights were as *blinding as a stage Klieg's*. No sooner did I adjust my eyes to the glare than a voice, cracking like a log in a fireplace, startled me to attention. In this atmosphere of fear, *I was no giant*; I was *more the dwarf*.

This is an improved version of the first mainly because the images are sharper. Such images as "moonlit" indicate little light; "like a squirrel's nut" shows how invisible the house really is until you come very close; "darkness covered me like a shroud" emphasizes the difficulty of seeing; "like a frozen shank of meat" the terror this person feels at this particular moment in time; "timidly" the unwillingness to go farther; "a massive, broad-beamed room" the incredible size of this strange room; "as blinding as a stage Klieg's" the intense glare; "cracking like a log in a fireplace" the deafening sound of the voice; "I was no giant" the lack of courage; "I was more like the dwarf" the fear that reduces the person to retreat.

Kinds of Images

There are several kinds of images. Each one has a form and a use all its own. Note the differences:

moonlit path	adjective description
like a squirrel's nut	simile
like a shroud	simile
timidly	adverb
massive broad-beamed room	adjective description
as blinding as a stage Klieg's	simile
cracking like a log in a fireplace	simile
I was no giant	metaphor
I was more the dwarf	metaphor

ADJECTIVE DESCRIPTION: AN ADJECTIVE CHARACTERIZING A PERSON OR THING

Examples: star-crossed lovers, big-boned player, Jack the Ripper, swift-footed deer

SIMILE: AN EXPRESSED COMPARISON BETWEEN TWO UNLIKE OBJECTS, USING LIKE OR AS

Examples: as black as tar, as ugly as a toad, pretty as a rose, built like a brick wall

ADVERBS: PARTS OF SPEECH THAT USUALLY ANSWER THE QUESTIONS HOW, WHEN, WHERE, OR WHY. THEY ARE IDENTIFIED EASILY BY THE "LY" ENDINGS, AND MODIFY VERBS.

Examples: snakily, hoveringly, devilishly, belligerently

METAPHOR: A FIGURE OF SPEECH IN WHICH TWO UNLIKE OBJECTS ARE COMPARED WITHOUT USE OF LIKE OR AS.

Examples: Your plan is a dead duck. The swimming pool is a cesspool. Vacations are heaven.

ASSIGNMENT

Write a paragraph description of a scene using specific adjective descriptions, similes, adverbs, and metaphors to create sharp images.

Procedure

How do you do this?

STEP 1: WRITE THE DESCRIPTION

First write it in straight prose just to get the idea developed. Then rewrite it making changes in language.

STEP 2: PREPARE AN OUTLINE

Suppose you have a very pretty backyard and wish to describe it so that the reader can visualize it. Think of three details about the backyard that are especially descriptive. Make a list of these features.

A Very Special Place
1. A giant maple tree towers over the house.
2. Redwood benches and chairs circle the grounds.
3. A big patio that reflects the sun.

STEP 3: CHANGE THE DETAILS INTO SPECIFIC IMAGES

Now you have to select the pictures that capture the maple tree, the redwood benches and chairs, and the big patio. Just how big is that tree? How wide a circle do those benches and chairs make? How big is the patio and just how intensely does it reflect the sun?

STEP 4: ADD CONCRETE IMAGES TO THE OUTLINE

A Very Special Backyard

1. A giant maple tree towers over the house like Gulliver in the land of Lilliputians
2. Wooden benches and chairs circle the ground
   wine red stain
   spaced like children dancing in a circle
3. A big patio that reflects the sun
   shaped like a baseball diamond
   the sun dances off the patio, making the shadows large

STEP 5: WRITE THE PARAGRAPH

With these word-pictures in mind, you can now begin the paragraph. You have planned the major phase of your writing. Now you must have an ending and a beginning.

STEP 6: READ YOUR TOPIC SENTENCE

That first line, the topic sentence, must be so appealing, so eye-catching, that the reader will be tempted to discover what is so unique about your backyard. Which one of the following possibilities best fits your subject?

1. Our expensive patio is the place where our family spends most of the time.

2. I love my patio and everything in it.

3. When you step through my kitchen door, you are in paradise.

If you chose No. 3, you were wise. While the other two are adequate as openers, the third draws the reader's attention to paradise. He may ask: "What does this paradise look like?" Now tell him with vivid pictures.

STEP 7: PUT IT ALL TOGETHER

A Very Special Place

When you step through my kitchen door, into the garden, you are in paradise. There, towering above you, like Gulliver in the land of Lilliputians, is a maple tree, a canvas of lovely color. Around the tree, like children dancing in a circle, are wooden benches and chairs. Their wine red stain is a pleasing sight on a bright summer day. Enclosing almost the entire grounds is a patio, shaped like a diamond, where the sun dances, making shadows leap. Relaxing here makes me feel at peace with the world. Isn't that what paradise is all about?

STEP 8: CONCLUDE

Note how the paragraph is completed. It is an effective closing because it restates the opening idea of paradise in a different way.

Exercise

In the following passage, identify the similes, metaphors, adverbs, and adjective descriptions that make the writing vivid and colorful:

> She wore a dark-striped dress reaching down to her shoe tops, and an equally long apron of bleached sugar sacks, with a full pocket: all neat and tidy, but everytime she took a step she might have fallen over her shoelaces, which dragged from her unlaced shoes. She looked straight ahead. Her eyes were blue with age. Her skin had a patina all its own of numberless branching wrinkles as though a whole little tree stood in the middle of her forehead; but a golden color ran underneath, and the two knobs of her cheeks were illumined by a yellow burning under the dark. Under the red rag her hair came down on her neck in the frailest of ringlets, still black, and with an odor like copper.

from "A Worn Path" by Eudora Welty

Follow-Up Exercise

Now try your hand at imagery. Write a paragraph on one of the following, using similes, metaphors, adverbial images, and adjective descriptions:

1. The animals at the zoo
2. The birds in my backyard
3. Sunset on the beach
4. Flying
5. Swimming underwater
6. A beautiful rainbow

HOW DO I USE ANALOGY IN MY WRITING?

(Credit: Wide World Photos.)

What analogy would you use to get the point across?

When you say "My father is as wise as Solomon," you are making an analogy. You are comparing your father's wisdom to a person in history who was known for great wisdom. Therefore, your father is understood to be extraordinarily wise. This analogy illustrates clearly the amount of wisdom your father has. Analogies help the reader to understand exactly what you are trying to say. Sometimes it is hard to pin down exactly what you want to get across. This is understandable because in the English language words have many meanings and the one you intend may not be the one the reader is getting. So, when you say "My neighbors are as rich as the Rockefellers," you help the reader to appreciate how vastly wealthy they are.

Analogies help to convey the exact meaning of a word or idea.

Books give you an understanding of life and people the way a flashlight illuminates a room. There is much in the printed word that helps us appreciate how people face problems and try to resolve them. A book is like a Boeing 747 that jets us quickly from place to place, from emotion to emotion, from action to action. Reading is like being led by a guide in a museum; books take us on tours of life and show us various parts of ourselves that we are not even aware of. Books may also remind us of the intellectual splendor of the great library at Alexandria, the genius of William Shakespeare, or the ideas of a great philosopher such as Nietzsche.

Analysis

The comparisons (analogies) made in the passage above help the reader to better appreciate the benefits of reading. Note the analogies and how they clarify ideas.

Analogy 1: books that light up the mind the way a flashlight lights the darkness

Analogy 2: books that enable us to travel the way a Boeing 747 transports us rapidly

Analogy 3: books that take us about the way a guide leads us through a museum

Analogy 4: books that offer ideas so splendid, like those offered by the most famous libraries or the most influential writers

Analogies to Render a Concept More Understandable

If you were writing about courage, beauty, truth, or love, it would be difficult to describe the abstract concept concretely, but using specific analogies would be helpful. For example, in describing the courage of a male oriole, one naturalist put it this way:

In defending his nest high in the trees, the male oriole fights furiously to protect the female and her chicks. He will beat his wings and thump them upon the branches while emitting so startling a sound that any marauding bird or animal most assuredly will retreat rather than take on this fearsome adversary. Just imagine Mohammad Ali being cornered in a ring and dancing out with precision and power, ringing his opponent with terrible blows. The picture of this giant smashing away should make you visualize the determination of the male oriole when compelled to make a stand. It is a scene of raw instinct that Nature alone views.

Analysis

The author compares the oriole's behavior toward an invader to the way the prizefighter Mohammad Ali fights his way out of a corner. The analogy to Mohammad Ali and his fighting prowess helps to make an otherwise unclear concept of bravery appreciated on human terms. This is an analogy that deepens our understanding of the oriole's courage.

Analogy to Make a Description More Vivid

My aunt is the most beautiful woman in the world. I say this with no exaggeration for everywhere she goes, people stop and stare in fascination. Her face radiates light and grace, her figure is like a classical statue, and her movements are as graceful as a swan's. Altogether, she is walking perfection, the ultimate of any artist's dream. When I think of my aunt I am reminded of the Greek masterpiece, the statue of Venus de Milo. The full-bodied curvature, the graceful stance, the combination of harmony and balance, all are the qualities this woman possesses. It's almost as if this creation has come to life and taken on the name of Sylvia Trent, my aunt.

Analysis

The comparison to a work of art that most people know and can identify as perfect beauty helps to convey the exquisite qualities of the writer's aunt. In other words, the status becomes the comparison point that makes the description of the woman more vivid.

Analogy To Make a Point of View More Convincing

Criminal laws should be enforced, even made stricter. As long as we permit criminals to get away, they are apt to repeat their crimes against society; and society, above all else, must be protected. A person who commits murder should lose his life, a person who rapes should be castrated, and a person who steals should be dealt with accordingly. In the old days, for example, thieves lost their hands and arsonists were burned. It may sound primitive to some but it is the only real way to deter those who find it tempting, or profitable, to take advantage of decent people.

Analysis

The writer's position on capital punishment is made more impressive by his reference to (or comparison with) justice in the past. Though we may not agree with his tactics, we do appreciate his position more clearly. Ancient law, here, acts as the reference point for his advocating sterner measures today.

Follow-Up Exercises

Now you are ready to use analogy in your own writing. When you develop your own ideas, consider what kind of comparison would be useful to make your writing more understandable.

1. How a certain problem should be solved

2. A person I admire greatly

3. An incident I'll never forget

4. A scene of great beauty

5. A trait I proudly possess

HOW DO I MAKE COMPARISONS?

(Credit: Nathan Farb.)

PROBLEM

You are asked to compare two things. How do you do this?

A *comparison* indicates similarities between two persons, two things, or two ideas. The purpose, then, is to show to what extent two persons, things, or ideas are closely related.

We make comparisons all the time. When you say, "My brother and I get along well together," you probably mean you both have a similar outlook and personality. If you thought about it, you could come up with a number of traits you both have that are similar. That process would be called *comparison*. Comparisons enable us to appreciate the value or quality of a particular person. For example, to say "Joe Merrick is smart" does not help us to appreciate how smart he is. But if we say, "Joe Merrick is as smart as the top student in the school," we have a better idea because we know what it takes to be the number one student in an entire school.

Comparisons can be:

Human: one person with another

Political: one party with another

Historical: one period of time with another

Life Experience: one event in your life with another

Physical: one location with another

Psychological: one state of mind with another

Geographical: one country with another

Social: one behavior with another

Educational: one class with another

Once we do this, set one person beside another, one period of time beside another, we are involved in comparison-making, and our purpose is to show similarities, not differences. (Contrasts show differences.)

Solution

Read the following passage and note: (1) who or what is being compared, (2) which qualities are being compared, and (3) how these similarities are organized.

A Trip to Russia

On my trip to the Soviet Union last summer, I discovered the Russian people to be open, honest, and friendly. In hotels, on buses, and in the street, many pedestrians stopped to greet me and discuss questions concerning how we live. When I inquired about how they live and what values are important to them, they responded honestly. In fact, one old man told me, "We like to have refrigerators and electric ovens, like you." On several occasions we were invited to join Russian families in their homes. Once we were actually hauled into a church to be part of a wedding. After the ceremony, we drank and ate with the people, danced, and plainly just had a good time. Unlike what I had thought before going to the Soviet Union, I observed that the ordinary people are very much like us Americans. Our reputation of being open about our feelings, honest about what we think, and friendly upon meeting strangers is not so very different from qualities of those Russian people I had the good fortune to meet. Maybe, when you get around the propaganda that governments feed us, all people are pretty much the same.

Evaluation

The Russian people and Americans are being compared.

1.   The three qualities of openness, honesty, and friendliness are focused on.

2.   The organization of these details involves the Russians first, then Americans.

3.   The purpose of this writing is to show to what extent both groups are similar; that is what we call a comparison.

Comparisons with a Different Organization

Another way of comparing, instead of doing one person and then the other, is to use the "point-by-point" method. In this case, you would make a point about a Russian, then compare it to an American. Note the differences in this version.

A Trip To Russia

On my trip to the Soviet Union last summer I discovered the Russian people to be open, honest, and friendly. In hotels, on buses, and in the street, many pedestrians stopped to greet me and discuss questions concerning how we live. Americans, too, have a way of coming right up to you and saying just what they think or feel openly. When I inquired about how Russians live and what values are important to them, they responded honestly. In fact, one old man told me, "We like to have refrigerators and electric ovens, like you." My American friends, of course, always refer to how easy life would be if only they had the money to buy all those machines to make their life easier. This materialistic outlook on life is not so surprising. On several occasions we were invited to join Russian families in their homes. Once we actually were hauled into a church to be part of a wedding. After the ceremony, we drank and ate with the people, danced, and plainly just had a good time. How many times, in America, have I been asked to join strangers out of sheer friendliness? Americans have always been especially reputed to be overly friendly, but unlike what I thought before going to the Soviet Union, the ordinary people there are very much like us. Our reputation of being open about our feelings, honest about what we think, and friendly upon meeting strangers is not so very different from qualities of those Russian people I had the good fortune to meet. Maybe, when you get around the propaganda that governments feed us, all people are pretty much the same.

Evaluation

The same Russians and Americans are being compared.

1.   The three qualities of openness, honesty, and friendliness are focused on.

2.   The organization of these details involves a point-by-point analysis: how Russians are open, how Americans are open; how Russians are honest, how Americans are honest; how Russians are friendly, how Americans are friendly.

3.   The purpose is the same: to show to what extent both groups are similar; a comparison has been used.

Of the two methods of comparison used, the details of one and then the details of another or the point-by-point approach, which one more effectively shows the closeness of the two peoples?

Follow-Up Exercise

Now make a comparison of your own, using either method.

1.   Two sports that require the same abilities

2.   Two people who are similar in character

3.   Two books that have the same theme or conflict

4.   Two events that had a similar effect on you

5.   Two historical periods that parallel each other

HOW DO I MAKE CONTRASTS?

(Credit: Wide World Photos.)

How would you contrast these two women?
What are the most obvious contrasts?

   In the previous chapter, you learned that a *comparison* matches qualities that are the same or similar. However, a *contrast* shows differences or dissimilarities. Your purpose in writing a contrast would be to point up how two things or two people are strikingly different.

Examples

Red and green are contrasting colors.

The movie version of *The Exorcist* may be contrasted with the book.

An Ivy League college may be contrasted with a community college.

Your parents may be different from other parents.

A particularly good teacher may be contrasted to a bad teacher.

A happy mood may be contrasted to a sad one.

ASSIGNMENT

Your teacher asks you to think of two people you know who are different. You are to contrast these to show specific differences.

How do you do this?

Procedure

STEP 1: MAKE A DECISION

Here you must choose two people you know well enough, but who represent very different traits. Who will they be?

STEP 2: OUTLINE THE QUALITIES OF THE TWO

Suppose you wish to show a superior teacher contrasted with one who is inferior. How would you outline this composition?

STEP 3: THE OUTLINE

Consider each teacher separately

1. Teacher A: Mr. Smith
   Outstanding traits
   A. He makes the subject interesting and real.
   B. He likes kids and relates to them warmly.
   C. He has a sense of humor that relaxes the class.

2. Teacher B: Mr. Jones
   Poor qualities
   A. He treats the students like babies.
   B. He is unpleasant, unfriendly, and sarcastic.
   C. He shows no understanding of teenage problems.

STEP 4: THINK THROUGH THE CONTRAST

Each detail of the teacher's character, as we have already learned, must be supported by a concrete example. Let us then refine the outline.

1. Teacher A: Mr. Smith, English teacher
   Outstanding traits
   A. He makes the subject interesting and real.
      Example: He asks us to give our personal feelings and values
   B. He likes kids and relates to them warmly.
      Example: He holds conferences after school to help individuals with work and problems.
   C. He has a sense of humor that relaxes the class.
      Examples: He tells funny stories about his family and his life.

2. Teacher B: Mr. Jones, Math teacher
   Poor qualities
   A. He treats the students like babies.
      Example: He repeats the work over and over and makes us copy everything word for word.
   B. He is unpleasant, unfriendly, and sarcastic.
      Example: He made a girl cry and leave the class.
   C. He shows no understanding of teenage problems.
      Example: He makes no allowance for make-up tests and demands the same quality work from everyone.

STEP 5: PUT IT TOGETHER

Remember, you are contrasting two teachers who are extremely unlike each other. Therefore, when you flesh this out, show them as extremes.

A Contrast in Attitude

It is amazing how two teachers working in the same school can be so different. Going from one class to the other is like journeying between the arctic and the tropics.

Mr. Smith, my English teacher, for example, is a study in expertise and good human relations. While the subject of English can be boring at times, this man devises ways to make it interesting and real. Whenever we discuss the actions of a character in a book, he challenges us with "How do you feel about what happened to this person?" You can see he likes kids from the way he relates warmly to them. As the period starts, he greets them at the door with a fond hello and after class he meets with some students to help them with problems. If kids need fun at times, then Mr. Smith is the man to relax them with funny jokes and humorous stories about his family and life.

On the other hand, there's Mr. Jones, my math teacher, who is everything Mr. Smith is not. To be in his class is to be forever a child in the way he repeats the work over and over and makes us copy material word for word.

All is serious study with no personal touch. All I can recall of that man is an unpleasant voice, an unfriendly frown, and a sarcastic attitude. Once, when a girl dared to question him on a certain theorem, he put her down so that she cried and left the class. Not once does Mr. Jones ever show an ounce of understanding of anyone's problems in class. Heaven help you if you are absent, even legitimately, because you can not even make up a missed test. Unfortunately, every student is treated the same, as if we were dolls on a shelf.

It is fun to be in Mr. Smith's exciting English class but sitting in Mr. Jones' math class is a horror all the time. How one can be so humane and the other so cruel is hard to understand. But I suppose that's part of growing up: learning how to exist with all kinds of people in this world.

STEP 6: CONCLUDE

The ending of a contrast composition, the right kind of ending, is as important as any other part of the writing. Reread this last paragraph and see whether or not it is a fitting way to close this contrast.

STEP 7: REVISE

Aside from any language errors you may pick up from checking through carefully, you are concerned with the overall purpose: to contrast two individuals for specific reasons so that the reader is clear about the differences.

STEP 8: EVALUATE

The way this paper is constructed we see very clearly not only how Mr. Smith is unlike Mr. Jones, but also how the writer feels about each. Feelings are always a nice touch if you can incorporate them smoothly. Note another point: The writer decided to do a portrait of one, then the other. Is this method an improvement over the point-by-point style?

Follow-Up Exercise

Now you can put together your own contrast. Try one of the following suggestions:

1. Where I live now compared to where I once lived

2. A good friend and a mere acquaintance

3. A magazine that puts the others to shame

4. A happy, outgoing person and one who is glum and withdrawn

5. One athletic team with another

HOW DO I USE DIALOGUE IN MY WRITING?

(Credit: Freelance Photographers Guild.)

What are these two saying to each other?
Can you imagine their dialogue?
How and When Do I Use Dialogue In My Writing?

ASSIGNMENT

Describe a scene with a friend, a family member, a teacher, or some important person in your life. In addition to describing the scene, include some examples of dialogue.

How do you go about doing this?

Procedure

You have two important tasks here. One is to select some person and tell about an important occasion with him or her. The second is to put into writing the actual words that were exchanged between the two of you.

Dialogue is a conversation between two or more individuals. This is nothing new, for we talk with people every day of our lives. We are constantly talking to other people and they are responding to us. We may be unconscious of this process but we are doing it all the time.

Writing this is another matter. We must capture the actual words that a person speaks, then write them on paper correctly. There are two ways of doing this:

Indirect: At the party, my friend asked me to go for an ice cream soda. I considered the offer and said I was not interested.

Direct: At the party, my friend asked me, "Want to go for an ice cream soda?"
I considered the offer and said, "No, thank you."

In the first case, the friend is being referred to as a third person, while in the second case we have the actual words that the friend spoke.

This is a quotation, not a dialogue. Dialogue occurs when there is a response to these words. For example:

At the party, my friend wanted to go for an ice cream soda and asked me, "Want to join me?"
I considered the offer and said, "No, thank you."

This is only a beginning. If you wish to build on this moment at the party, you may add what your friend said in answer to your refusal. A fuller treatment of this scene may go something like this:

At the party, my friend asked me, "Want to go for an ice cream soda?"
I considered the offer and said, "No, thank you."
"Why not?" he asked.
I tried to be honest. "Because I don't particularly care for ice cream."
"I don't believe it," he answered. "I thought everyone is crazy about ice cream."
"Well, here's one who isn't," I told him calmly.
I could see he was disappointed.
"Okay, another time, I guess," he said in parting.

If you include this conversation in the larger description of the scene of the party, you are adding realism and interest because dialogue spices up writing. Just telling what happened is not always as effective as offering the actual words used. Writers do this all the time. Study the excerpts below.

Examples

In the novel *Of Human Bondage* by W. Somerset Maugham:

"Had a bath this morning?" Thompson said when Philip came to the office late, for his early punctuality had not lasted.

"Yes, haven't you?"

"No, I'm not a gentleman, I'm only a clerk. I have a bath on Saturday night."

"I suppose that's why you're more than usually disagreeable on Monday," Philip observed.

In the one-act play "The Mother" by Paddy Chayefsky:

Daughter: "Ma, why don't you come live with George and me?"
Old Lady: "No, no, Annie, you're a good daughter..."
Daughter: "We'll move Tommy into the baby's room, and you can have Tommy's room. It's the nicest room in the apartment. It gets all the sun..."
Old Lady: "I have three wonderful children. I thank God every night for that."

In the short story "The White Circle" by John Bell Clayton:

Then he said quietly, "I don't ever want anyone ever to touch this trip rope or to have occasion to step inside this circle."

So that was why I didn't now look up toward the fork.

"I don't want to play no sissy prisoner's base," Anvil said.

"All right," I lied. "I know where there's a nest. But one game of prisoner's base first."

"You don't know where there's any pigeon nest," Anvil said.

In all these excerpts, the writers have recorded precisely words being used in conversation. They don't guess or interpret what a character may be saying; they convey the thoughts and actions of the character directly through speech. The readers can interpret for themselves what the characters feel.

This is the trick in using dialogue effectively. Going back to the original assignment, which is to write about an experience with another person, your paper might look something like this:

Being Honest with Yourself

When the invitation to a party at Jack's house came, I was so excited I yelled, "Fantastic!" There were three days until Saturday, but I counted every one. In my head I kept saying, "One, two, three," as if I were keeping a scorecard.

Then the party came and I was there with all my friends — those I knew in school and some strangers, friends of Jack's. One of them, seeing me enter, walked up and introduced himself.

"Hi, I'm Fred Horn, Jack's friend from camp."

I shook his hand. "I'm Leon Jarris, Jack's school friend."

"Yeah, I know," Fred said. "He's told me about your track record."

"Just like Jack," I responded, "always sounding off about his friends."

"A great guy, Jack, don't you think?" he asked.

"None better," I answered as I walked to meet the others.

Later, while the party was well under way, the music and voices mingling loudly, joints were passed around and everyone smoked. When it came my turn, I passed it on to the person next to me. I was a little embarrassed but I was scared of repeating what had happened the week before.

Fred Horn, who joined me on the couch, wanted to get high and asked me, "Want to join me?"

I considered the offer and said, "No, thank you."

"Why not?" he asked.

I tried to be honest. "Because I had a bad scene last week, when I mixed alcohol and pot."

"Ah, it couldn't happen again," my friend insisted. "Try it."

"I really don't want to," I pleaded.

I could see he was disappointed. "Okay, man, stay cool."

I did for the rest of the evening but I was out of the action. At the end of the party, as everybody was leaving, Jack asked, "Hey, did you have a good time, Leon?"

"Sure did," I lied. "It was the best of parties."

If you look at this passage carefully, you will see that it (1) describes a particular event at a party, (2) deals with how a person feels in a certain situation, and (3) is written so that the reader gets the sense of a past event firsthand. The writer has not told about the scene; he has presented it. The reader gets the impression of something real.

When used sparingly, dialogue is very effective. It must not be overused, misused, or even underused. You, the writer, must decide when people talking to each other will enliven the situation. Perhaps the best rule of thumb is to insert dialogue when you want the character's interactions with others to show. Is he or she honest? Is there affection between the characters? When used in this way, properly placed dialogue makes a total piece of writing much more dramatic.

The Technical Use of Dialogue

Dialogue form requires a knowledge of quotation marks, their use and placement. The quotation mark is a precise tool that must be applied correctly.

Rule 1: Use the quotation mark to indicate *exact* words spoken by a person, for example: "Come here," the teacher said, "and give me the paper."

Rule 2: It is placed before the first word spoken and after the punctuation at the end, for example: The man yelled, "Stop that car!"

Rule 3: If the words spoken are interrupted in the middle, then two sets of quotation marks are required, for example: "I wish you would help me," I said, "instead of hindering me."

The words "I said" come in the middle of the entire quotation and break it in two — therefore we need two sets of quotation marks.

Rule 4: Each time a new person speaks, begin a new paragraph; otherwise the reader will be confused as to who is talking.

My mother called out, "Clean the table, John, and wash it down."
"Yes, Mother," I answered.

Exercise

The following dialogue is unpunctuated. Using what you have learned about quotation marks, place them properly around the words actually spoken.

I walked into the house and called out what's for supper? My mother turned from the stove to say steak and potatoes. No I don't like steak and potatoes so I answered damn it. Clearly my mother was annoyed but she tried not to show it. Instead, she embraced me warmly and said welcome home, Fred. I hope you had a good day.

I kissed her and placed my books on the table. You know, Mother, I confessed, I may complain a lot but I think you're the greatest.

I love you too she answered but you complain too much.

Follow-Up Exercise

To practice writing dialogue, select one of the following situations and, using quotations, write a scene in which the two speak to each other:

1. A talk with a teacher about a mark

2. I help my friend with a problem

3. An employer interviews me for a job

4. A fight with my brother

5. My mother refuses to let me stay out late at night

6. A conversation with a stranger on a bus

7. A chat with my next-door neighbor

Chapter Five

TECHNIQUES THAT DEVELOP STRUCTURE AND CLARITY

How often have you heard your teacher comment, "Your writing is not clear." Or "Your ideas are not very coherent." Or "You lack unity in this composition." In this chapter, you learn the skills that make writing clear, coherent, unified. You will practice techniques that enable you to show relationships such as cause and effect, use details to support a general statement, or take steps to build a climax. Read the sections carefully and take note of the specific techniques for effective communication.

HOW CAN I IMPROVE THE STRUCTURE?

I love sports. They are exciting. They give me pleasure. Especially football. It is a contact sport, we play it all the time.

What is wrong with these sentences? How would you improve them?

Sentences are the basic units of writing. They are the building blocks that cement the ideas you are expressing. When you put a number of them together, you have what is called a paragraph. (Three or more of these paragraphs together make up a composition or essay.) Sentences, then, are like the pillars of a bridge. Without them, the bridge would topple; but when they are solid, the bridge stands firm. Think of the top of the bridge as the idea part of your writing, the pillars as the supporting sentences that hold up the overall idea.

Bridge: The Overall Idea

PILLAR 1

SENTENCE 1

PILLAR 2

SENTENCE 2

PILLAR 3

SENTENCE 3

PILLAR 4

SENTENCE 4

PILLAR 5

SENTENCE 5

This is a well-constructed bridge because it is supported by pillars that are unified and strongly imbedded. Each pillar (sentence) is composed in such a way that the bridge (the overall idea) lies straight and does not sag. The person who plans his sentences in such a way will always convey clear meanings to the reader.

But what happens when the pillars (the sentences) are not so well-structured? The bridge (the overall idea) leans over or even collapses.

PILLAR 1

SENTENCE 1

PILLAR 2

SENTENCE 2

PILLAR 3

SENTENCE 3

PILLAR 4

SENTENCE 4

PILLAR 5

SENTENCE 5

Such a poor bridge (development of an idea) can only happen when the writer composes weak pillars (sentences). The answer, then, to good, clear, effective writing is arranging fully developed, complete sentence units that work together to support and sustain a general idea.

Example of a Weak Bridge

It happened when I was five years old, my family and I went on a trip to Vermont. Where the skies are clear and blue and the mountains sky-high. We were all ready to go, so we left early. My mother, two brothers, and I left Monday morning. My father joined us a week later. The trip itself was a long one, we were exhausted when we got to our summer home. A nice place to relax in.

Evaluation

The way the sentence units are written here, the bridge (the idea of traveling a long way to a summer home and arriving exhausted) sags terribly. It is not a bridge a reader can travel comfortably.

PILLAR 1:

It happened when I was five years old, my family and I went on a trip to Vermont.

Run-on sentence: Separating these two ideas by a comma confuses the meaning. Since they are related, they should be connected to show a relationship.

Correction: It happened when I was five years old, *when* my family and I went on a trip to Vermont.

PILLAR 2:

Where the skies are clear blue and the mountains sky-high.

Sentence fragment: By itself, this sentence fragment is unclear because the reader is unsure where such a sky and mountains are. In other words, there is no subject or reference point.

Correction: When I was five years old, my family and I went on a trip to Vermont *where* the skies are clear blue and the mountains sky-high.

PILLAR 3:

We were all ready to go, so we left early.

Poorly subordinated sentence: If leaving early depends on being ready, then the sentence fails to show that relationship.

Correction: *Since* we were all ready, we left early.

PILLAR 4:

My mother, my two brothers, and I left Monday morning. My father joined us a week later.

Poorly coordinated sentence: The two ideas, the family's leaving and the father's leaving are given no connection here. Instead, they are written as separate ideas.

Correction: My mother, my two brothers, and I left Monday morning, *while* my father joined us a week later.

PILLAR 5:

The trip itself was a long one, we were exhausted when we got to our summer home.

The run-on sentence: Here again the separation of the idea of the long trip and the exhaustion upon arrival creates confusion as to the relationship.

Correction: *Because* the trip itself was a long one, we were exhausted when we got to our summer home.

PILLAR 6:

A nice place to relax in.

Sentence fragment: Obviously the thought is incomplete and unconnected to anything else. The reader wonders, *"What* is a nice place to relax in?"

> Correction: Because the trip itself was a long one, we were exhausted when we got to our summer home, *which* is a nice place to relax in.

Now the bridge (the overall idea) is rebuilt because we made the pillars (the sentences) firmer. Notice the vast improvement:

> When I was five years old, my family and I went on a trip to Vermont where the skies are clear blue and the mountains sky-high. Since we were all ready, we left early. My mother, my two brothers, and I left Monday morning, while my father joined us a week later. Because the trip itself was a long one, we were exhausted when we got to our summer home, which is a nice place to relax in.

Evaluation

The six pillars (the sentence units) are now positioned in such a way that the bridge (the idea of a trip taken by a family) is smooth, even, and understandable.

Exercise

Now read the following passage and note how the writer builds his bridge of ideas. Can you recognize which sentences are sturdy pillars?

My Favorite Pastime

> Since I love everything about cars, I adore collecting them. Whenever I get a chance, I visit antique car shows to search for a beauty that I can own and rebuild. This hobby of mine, which is not popular with my family, keeps me very busy. In fact, it takes me away from other duties and jobs because I have no time for anything else. While other people get their kicks from stamp collecting or raising pets, I get mine from this involvement with old cars. As few others I know take such an interest in this hobby, I do not share my joy.

Evaluation

Note how ideas are connected by such conjunctions as "since," "whenever," "which," "because," "while," and "as." They help to make one idea relate to or follow from another clearly and logically.

Follow-Up Exercise

Now build your own bridge on solid pillars. Avoid run-on sentences, sentence fragments, and poorly coordinated sentences.

BRIDGE

You wish to persuade your principal that a smoking lounge is needed in your school.

Pillar 1: Many youngsters smoke anyway. They need a place where they can relax and feel comfortable.

Pillar 2: It is true smoking may be harmful to one's health. Students have the right to decide.

Pillar 3: There is a high incidence of cutting in the school. A smoking lounge would keep students inside.

Pillar 4: The school is filthy with butts all over the floor. The lounge would contain them in one area.

Line up your pillars and construct a solid bridge of writing.

HOW DO I DECIDE WHICH POINT OF VIEW TO USE?

(Credit: Jay Lurie. From Freelance Photographers Guild.)

What point of view is expressed in this scene?
Whose point of view is it?

How Do I Decide Which Point of View To Use?

ASSIGNMENT

Relate an incident in a person's life. Decide which point of view to use.

How do you do this?

Points of View

There are basically four points of view to choose from. They are: Personal Involved, Personal Subjective, Personal Objective, and Omniscient.

1. *Personal Involved* would be used only if the incident you are relating involves you. In other words, if you were going to choose some incident from your own life, of which you were a part, then you would be writing it from the *Personal Involved* point of view.

2. *Personal Subjective* would be used if you are relating an incident as an observer who is dealing with feelings, rather than recording the facts as they happened.

3. *Personal Objective* would be used if your incident occurred to someone else but you were there as a witness. In other words, you were not directly affected but you were there.

4. *Omniscient* ("all-knowing") would be used to relate someone else's experience when you were not there. In other words, you may have heard about this and were so impressed with what happened you wanted to put down on paper what you heard or read.

EXAMPLE 1: PERSONAL INVOLVED

> While *I was swimming* the storm broke. Claps of thunder shook the sky as *I leaped from the cold lake and raced up the bank to a sheltering tree.* There, *I curled under the branches and tried to shield my body with my arms, leaning hard against the trunk.* The rain poured down so heavily *I was unable to move* out of the protection of the huge maple tree. *I sat and waited* for the storm to abate.

The writer of this passage tells the incident of the storm from his own experience as he remembers it. *He himself* was caught in this storm, and therefore the point of view is *Personal Involved*. The underlined parts are the clues of this personal involvement. You can tell from the use of the pronoun "I" and the directness of the action.

EXAMPLE 2: PERSONAL SUBJECTIVE

> *I watched* my brother win the big race. From the sidelines *I could see* the entire race well, and *I knew,* as *I sat there,* he would outdistance his competitors. As Bill leaped from the starting line, *I yelled* with frenzy to goad him on. Even when he crossed the tape, ahead of the others, *I couldn't stop cheering.* Then, *how proud I was to watch* my brother the athlete receive his trophy.

The writer here tells about a day when his brother was victorious in a race. This writer is there, seeing everything, but he's not involved. It is his brother, not he, who is performing the action. Therefore, we can see the point of view of this passage is *Personal Subjective*, subjective because the observer is dealing with his feelings rather than recording the facts as they happened.

EXAMPLE 3: OMNISCIENT OBSERVER

The bird seemed to be feeding on some worm when the cat stalked in from the bushes. The bird, unaware of the approacher, kept its beak in the ground, while the cat inched forward, slowly, surely. Just when the cat was about to leap upon its prey, the feathered creature flew up in terrible fright in just enough time to escape.

The way the writer conveys the suspense of that moment is recorded as one might have observed it, but without personal emotions. We know what was happening only because the writer recorded it objectively for us. It's almost like a filmed sequence. This may be considered an *Omniscient* point of view.

If we were to take the same scene and change it slightly, we would have another point of view. Note what happens.

EXAMPLE 4: PERSONAL OBJECTIVE

I was watching a bird feeding on some worms when a cat stalked in from the bushes. It seemed *to me* that the bird was unaware of its approacher, so busily did its beak work into the ground. *I noticed* the cat inch forward, slowly, surely. Just when the cat was about to leap upon its prey, I beheld the feathered creature fly up in a terrible fright in just enough time, I *felt*, to escape.

The use of the first person "I" changes the perspective. The difference in this passage is that the writer-observer indicates his position, his manner of seeing, and even how he felt. This may be called *Personal Objective*.

Knowing which point of view to use in your writing is extremely important, but which one you adopt depends on (1) whether or not you are personally involved, (2) whether or not you are a distant observer, (3) whether or not you are just describing or recording a scene, and (4) whether or not you are telling about an incident in which you were present.

PROBLEM

Which point of view would be best for each of the following?

1. An accident you saw

2. A time you got lost

3. An incident in your mother's life

4. Watching a friend win an award at graduation

5. Observing the snow fall

Now back to your assignment. Suppose you are very impressed with a recollection your mother has of her childhood, one she has retold many times. The account of what happened to her has remained in your mind and you can actually imagine it as if you were there. So you feel you want to write about it. Which point of view would it be? The *Omniscient* one is probably best.

STEP 1: OUTLINE THE NARRATIVE

My mother found a thousand dollars in a wallet.
1. She brought it home first to decide what to do.
2. She was tempted to keep it.
3. She noticed an address with a name.
4. She decided to return it.
5. When she got there, the owner turned out to be blind.
6. She felt so good and proud of being honest.

STEP 2: WRITE FROM THE OMNISCIENT POINT OF VIEW

Since this is not your own experience, the proper way is to use the third person "she" rather than the first person "I." It happened to her, remember, not to you.

STEP 3: ORGANIZE IT ACCORDING TO OUTLINE

Are the details in the right chronological (time) order? If so, then you are ready to proceed.

STEP 4: PROVIDE TRANSITIONS

From one detail to another, remember to use transitional words like "nevertheless," "however," "for example," "then," and so forth. This technique helps to add variety and zest to your style.

STEP 5: THINK OF A SUITABLE ENDING

The concluding statement is as important as anything else you write, for it flavors the writing and gives it meaning.

STEP 6: THE ACTUAL WRITING

When all the previous steps have been prepared, you are ready to convey that scene from the past. It may look like this:

> My mother, when she was sixteen years old, found a thousand dollars in a wallet lying on the street. Pleased as she was, she brought it home first to decide what to do. First she was tempted to keep it and spend it on so many wonderful things she desired, but then she noticed an address card with a name written on it. Naturally, she was embarrassed about keeping so much money when there was a person who might need the money for something far more important. This guilt, therefore, made her decide to return it. When she got to the address, she found an old man reclining on a couch. As he spoke, he barely looked her way, and his voice was faint and weak. In addition, she discovered that he was totally blind and quite helpless. Even as she handed the money to him, she felt a lot better. Further, when the blind old man offered her a reward for her honesty, she refused. The deed of making a helpless human being happy was reward enough.

Such an account gives us a warm, personal picture of the writer's mother at some important moment in her life. This is an effective use of the *Omniscient* point of view.

Follow-Up Exercise

Now compose your own account, using one of the following: *Personal Involved, Personal Subjective, Personal Objective,* or *Omniscient*.

1. An accident you saw

2. A time you got lost

3. Watching a friend win an award at graduation

4. Observing the snow fall

5. Being a witness to a mugging or a robbery

HOW DO I WRITE COHERENTLY?

(Credit: Leo de Wys, Inc.)

What is coherent about this scene?

ASSIGNMENT

In one paragraph, describe a scene in which you use three specific details coherently.

Why is it necessary to write coherently?

Sentences that are linked together in such a way that the reader can follow them clearly and logically help us make a coherent statement.

The following is an example of a paragraph that is *not* coherent:

> I was fortunate recently to visit a great museum, the Museum of Modern Art. I was led to see the painting "Guernica" by Pablo Picasso. It is a huge painting that hangs right in front of the entrance to a room. I stood there and studied the figures. On the painting there were people looking up in fright and anguish. Other parts had animals and houses that looked destroyed. The colors are bright and intense and capture one's attention. The entire painting gives one the impression that war is the most terrible tragedy that can happen to a country. Pablo Picasso created this work to remind the world of the cruelty of war.

When you read this paragraph, you have a sense that the writer had an important experience in discovering a great work of art, but the way it is written is not smooth and connected. What is needed is coherence.

The following is an example of a paragraph that is coherent, by means of transitional (connecting) words that carry one thought into another connected thought to show a relationship.

Example

> Recently, I was fortunate enough to visit a great museum, the Museum of Modern Art. When I arrived there, I was led immediately to see "Guernica" by Pablo Picasso. It is a huge painting that hangs right in front of the entrance to a room. After I studied it from a distance awhile, I moved close, until I could stand and study the figures. Shockingly, there are people looking up in fright and anguish in the painting. In another area there are animals and houses that look destroyed. In addition, the colors are bright and intense, almost jarring, and thus call attention to sharp contrasts. Overall, the entire painting gives one the impression that war is painful and disrupting — the most terrible tragedy that can happen to a country. Undoubtedly, Pablo Picasso created this work to remind the world of the cruelty of war.

This is an account of the same experience but it is a much better one. It is better because the writer has established relationships between the ideas, by using transitional words and phrases, such as: *when I arrived there, recently, immediately, after I moved closer, shockingly, in addition, thus, overall,* and *undoubtedly*. These words act as links from one thought to another, and thus make the meaning clearer.

Other transitional, or linking, expressions are: however, nevertheless, yet, there, thereafter, for instance, for example, after, then, and first.

Solution

Now back to your assignment. You are asked to compose a paragraph that contains specific details presented coherently.

STEP 1: THINK OF A FOCUS

Ask yourself: "What do I know well enough to describe in detail?"

STEP 2: MAKE A DECISION

You may be thinking of a friend, a pet, a teacher, a room, a car. But the decision depends on how well you know this person, creature, or object.

Your list may look like this:

My Best Friend

The Pet I Love

My Favorite Teacher

My Own Room

The Car that I Drive

Ask yourself: "Which one can I describe well enough so the reader can understand?"

STEP 3: MAKE THE OUTLINE

Suppose you have chosen "The Pet I Love." Now think of three key details that may be used to describe this particular pet.

Detail 1: My dog Shag is cuddly and loves to snuggle close.

Detail 2: She is spoiled and pampered by the whole family.

Detail 3: Whenever she spots another dog she gets nervous and growls.

STEP 4: FLESH OUT THE DETAILS AND EXPLAIN THEM

All key words must be developed, such as "cuddly," "snuggle," "spoiled," "pampered," and "nervous."

STEP 5: ELABORATE ON A DETAIL

Detail 1: My dog Shag is cuddly and loves to snuggle close. A tiny West Highland terrier, she finds her way to any soft spot, including people's legs and arms. Whenever I sit down in my playroom, she jumps up and sticks her head into my lap.

Detail 2: She is spoiled and pampered by the whole family. My sister always feeds her food from the dinner table. My brother also allows her to sleep on his bed at night. As a result, she is unhappy when she has to sleep alone.

Detail 3: Whenever she spots another dog she gets nervous and growls. With people she is calm and easy, but with animals her body trembles and she becomes tense and alert. The reason for all this is probably because we keep her in the house all the time and have not trained her to go outside alone.

STEP 6: WRITE THE TOPIC SENTENCE

Since this is to be a paragraph, you must begin with a sentence that captures the main, overall idea.

My beloved Shag, a West Highland terrier, is cuddly, spoiled, and nervous.

In this opening line, you have established what it is you love, and you have stated three qualities of the pet.

STEP 7: PUT IT ALL TOGETHER

Since the point of all this writing is putting ideas together coherently, you should consider how you will bridge the three details. Think of which transitional expressions (when, thus, moreover, therefore, etc.) will apply in making the writing smooth.

My Favorite Pet

My beloved Shag, a West Highland terrier, is cuddly, spoiled, and nervous. She just loves, for example, to find her way to any soft spot and to snuggle close to people's legs and arms. Whenever I sit down in the den, she jumps up and squeezes her head into my lap. In addition to this peculiarity, Shag thrives on the pampering she receives from the whole family. For instance, we all feed her human, instead of dog, food. Most of the time, my brother and I allow her to sleep on our beds instead of confining her to the kitchen. We do this because we love her, not because it is especially good for her. She is, as a result, so spoiled that she has trouble relating to other dogs. Lately, whenever she spots another animal she rises on her hind legs and growls. Overall, she is an unpredictable creature that can be both calm and fidgety, relaxed and tense. Like people, Shag can be a nuisance, but I love her all the same.

Note the underlined transitional expressions which help to convey the picture of the dog in a smooth manner.

Follow-Up Exercise

Use three details to describe one of the following topics. Organize them in an interesting and coherent way.

1. My best friend
2. My favorite teacher
3. My own room

4. The car I drive
5. The street where I live
6. A popular place for kids

HOW DO I SUPPORT A GENERAL STATEMENT?

(Credit: John Robaton. From Leo de Wys, Inc.)

State the general idea you get from this picture.
State three specific details that support the general statement.

Examples of General Statements

1. We should continue our space program.

2. Too many kids of this generation are on drugs.

3. Schools are failing students in reading and writing skills.

4. Jimmy Carter will turn out to be a better president than Gerald Ford.

5. The book *The Exorcist* is a much better story than the film.

6. Capital punishment should be abolished entirely.

These statements, if you examine them carefully, are opinions, and as opinions they have limitations. To think or believe that something is true or false, to make a conclusion, or to interpret a situation, is all right, but you must support the thinking, the belief, or the interpretation. For example, let us develop the opinions above.

1. Why should we continue the space program? In what ways is our space program an advantage over no space program at all?

2. How many kinds? Which drugs? What are the reasons?

3. What proof is there that reading and writing skills are falling off? Which tests or surveys give such information?

4. In what way will he be better? In which area — domestic, international, national?

5. What is meant by "better"? Is it the acting, the writing, the style, the suspense, the description?

6. Why would it be better to do away with capital punishment? And if we do, how will criminals be treated?

PROBLEM

How Do I Support My Facts?

All of these questions indicate that the original statements are incomplete and much too general. If they are to have any meaning, they must be supported by facts, statistics, references, quotes, or any other objective information.

How do you do this?

Example of an Opinion That Has No Support or Convincing Arguments

I believe that capital punishment should be abolished because executing murderers is murder itself. Besides, what does it accomplish to have an execution when the victim is already dead? Another reason is that it's expensive to keep a murderer on death row for a long period of time. I don't believe capital punishment prevents serious crime anyway because murders still go on. Just read the newspaper any day to see how many murders are committed in big cities. What I would like to see is a way to rehabilitate major criminals so that, at some time in their lives, they can see the error of their ways. This makes more sense than placing them in the electric chair.

Evaluation

This position on capital punishment is very general, full of opinion, but has no supporting evidence to make the writer's views convincing. It lacks support.

Solution

Now read the same position with more concrete support.

I believe the time has come to abolish capital punishment because the execution of criminals is itself murder. The governor of Arkansas, in a recent address, had this to say: "It is with great regret that I, upholding the penal code of this state, must sign writs of execution, inasmuch as I see no purpose whatsoever to taking a prisoner's life in the name of law." Besides, what does it accomplish to execute a murderer when the victim is already dead and cannot be restored to life? Even families of murdered people have testified that they would prefer to see the murderers of their loved ones live out their days in regret. One such parent, after sitting through a trial in New Jersey, said, "Nothing can restore my daughter to me. Better the murderer should live long enough to repent his terrible act." Another reason is that it is too expensive to keep a murderer on death row for a long period of time. In the state of Georgia, at least a dozen such murderers are awaiting executions at terrible expense. It is estimated that the cost to the state of Georgia is $20,000 a year for each such person. I don't believe capital punishment prevents a serious crime anyway because murders still go on. The Federal Bureau of Investigation has issued a report stating that, if anything, crimes of murder have increased in some parts of the country, notably in states where there is a capital punishment law. The Justice Department reveals, in a recent finding, the high incidence of murder in big metropolitan areas such as New York and Chicago. Just read the paper any day to see how many murders are committed in big cities. In one recent edition, I discovered three cases of murder. What I would like to see is a way to rehabilitate major criminals so that, at some time in their lives, they can see the error of their ways. Jason Richards, convicted of murder at the age of 17 and released from prison at the age of 37, has been restored to a normal way of life. He even said, in a press interview, "Spending all that time in prison has helped me to see the love of God." Such a view, helping murderers to atone for horrible acts and maybe placing them back in society, makes more sense than placing them in the electric chair.

If you note the underscored lines, you will see very specific support that strengthens each general statement. In the second version, the person's views are much more convincing.

Other Forms of Writing With Supporting Details

In description you must also present certain concrete details that develop your general idea. These are not facts or statistics but examples that help the reader to understand how you feel about a person, a scene, or an object.

Read the following passage and note how this writer takes an idea and develops it in such a way that you really grasp it fully:

A Very Special Season

October is that time of the year when the world is beautiful in a special way. The barns are brimming with produce, the hay is piled sky-high, and the wine runs oozy red in the vineyards. Bees bore into their nests, birds change homes, and insects crawl crazily in circles as the sun plummets in red streaks. Ah, those autumn leaves sparkle in mantles of color and when they fall they stir the air with graceful dancing. A look into a farm pantry will reveal jarred sweets, canned vegetables, and preserved meats — all arranged in handsome and careful order. The smell of horses lazing in the field makes one want to leave the world of neverending toil. There is a blaze of refreshing vision as one kicks knobs of fallen wood against the banks of ferns only to arouse mouselike creatures beginning their winter rest. What wonders the month of October brings to weary souls and tired eyes.

The first sentence makes the impression clear. Each of the following sentences adds another dimension to that view of October's special beauty. Some appeal to our sense of sight, while others arouse our hearing, touch, or smell. Such supporting sensory highlights help to make the picture of the world in October a very special, beautiful one.

In narration, too, supporting the event with specific details is essential. The kinds of details you include help to support the effect you wish to create. For example, in this short narrative sequence, note the three supporting details that further the movement of the scene:

I was never so scared of the night as I was yesterday. As I was walking home from my friend's house, a strange figure hurtled toward me and made me start with fright. There, in front of me, stood a seven-foot monster cloaked in a black bag, its eyes stretching out of their sockets. Blood poured from the nose and ran like a stream down the chin. I braced myself against the side of the building and clutched the cold brick in my hands. I felt trapped on the very street where I lived. Even the moon, normally out to light my way, had deserted me in my worst moment. The grotesque figure reached out to grab me; at the same time an alley cat wailed in the grass. I sank to the ground, pleading, "Please, please, let me go. I promise I won't stay out late anymore."

We can all be scared, but each person's fright is different depending on the circumstances. The writer of this frightening episode stirs our own fear by building on (1) a strange figure appearing out of nowhere, (2) a familiar street that suddenly seemed to be dangerous, and (3) the feel of a cold wall and the screech of a cat. All these details add to the mood of fright that the writer captures.

Whenever you make a statement in writing, always:

1. Explain it fully.

2. State it clearly.

3. Support it with details, whether you are describing, narrating, or arguing a point of view.

Follow-Up Exercise

Select one of the following general ideas and support it with three solid details:

1. I really believe there is a communication gap between parents and kids.

2. There will never be a major, all-out war between the U.S. and Russia.

3. The abortion law in our state should be abolished.

4. Jimmy Carter will be a great president.

5. Marijuana should be legalized.

6. Exercise is the best way to maintain health.

HOW DO I USE SPECIFIC INFORMATION IN MY WRITING?

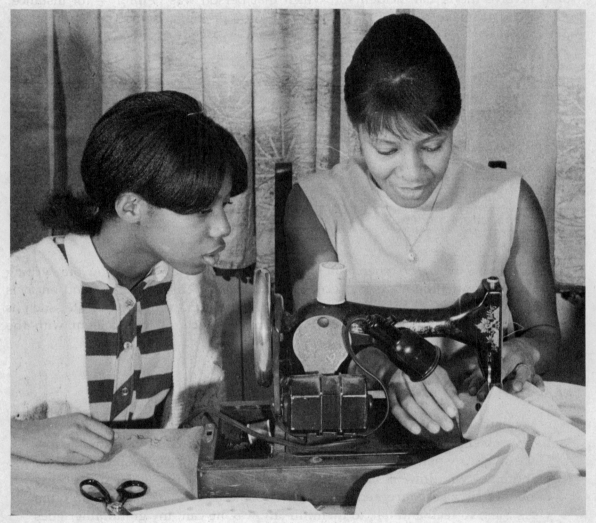

(Credit: Leo de Wys, Inc.)

What is happening in this picture? Be specific.

ASSIGNMENT

Your teacher asks you to take a position on capital punishment and to support the position with specific reasons. How do you do this?

In writing, all general or topic statements should be supported by specific information. This is the ideal way to develop ideas. You can avoid a poorly written paragraph or essay by planning for relevant details and illustrations. For example, if you are planning to write about how important it is to communicate with people, it would be helpful to think of specific ways people really communicate with one another — for example, by writing, by speaking, by showing interest and attention. If you are thinking of writing about a person who helped you in some way, the specifics would involve the actual incidents in which that person was helpful — for instance, guiding you to make a decision, listening to your problem, or maybe lending you money when you needed it.

Kinds of Specific Information

There are four types of specifics that you should know. They are:

1. Examples and illustrations

2. Facts, statistics, and data

3. Incidents and experiences

4. Reasons

How you use these, or when you use them, depends on what you are writing about. If you are writing about our economy, you would, of course, depend on facts and statistics. On the other hand, if you are describing an event in your life, such as an accident, you would be expected to combine the facts of the accident with the experience you had.

EXAMPLE 1: USING EXAMPLES AND ILLUSTRATIONS

> My grandfather is an extremely generous man in many ways. When people have problems, he gives his time to share their concern and help them cope. For example, when my father needed capital to start a new business, my grandfather withdrew money from his own bank account and lent it to my father. He is also concerned with older people in old age homes; he often visits them to read and talk to them. In any way he can, my grandfather goes to extremes to be of assistance to those in need.

The general statement of the grandfather's generosity is made more specific by the examples of sharing problems, lending money, and the illustration of volunteer work for other, less fortunate aged people.

EXAMPLE 2: USING FACTS, STATISTICS, DATA

> Smoking among teenagers is on the increase. In 1971, 10 per cent of the age group between 14 and 18 smoked cigarettes. In 1977, that number tripled.

The National Cancer Society, in its 1976 study of teenage smoking, indicated a rise of more than seven per cent a year in the frequency of the smoking habit, especially among youngsters 14 and under. A poll in my own school shows that for every 10 nonsmokers, there are at least 3 who are habitual users of cigarettes. Unquestionably, for whatever reasons, smoking among young people is on the rise.

Note the use of hard data to support the position that more young people are smoking today: "10 per cent of the age group between 14 and 18," "a rise of more than 7 per cent a year," "for every 10 nonsmokers there are at least 3 who are habitual users of cigarettes." The use of such facts makes the general statement convincing and not just a matter of opinion.

EXAMPLE 3: USING INCIDENTS AND EXPERIENCES

I have always been terribly afraid of heights. Being high up makes me dizzy and I soon lose consciousness. Once my father took me to the top of the Empire State Building, which overlooks the skyline of New York City. Looking down at the antlike people below, I felt I was falling through a great distance. Another time, at the rim of the Grand Canyon, while taking pictures of a sunset, I lost my footing. Still another instance occurred while I was sunbathing on the roof of my building: I almost reeled over the edge. Heights are certainly not for me, nor will I ever allow myself to be in such a potentially dangerous situation again.

The writer's fear of heights (acrophobia) is supported well with specific incidents that make it more understandable and therefore convincing. The instances of standing atop the Empire State Building, the Grand Canyon, and the roof of the building are excellent choices to develop this particular fear.

EXAMPLE 4: USING REASONS

I really believe everybody should learn to type. It's certainly faster than writing, and therefore you can get a lot more done in a shorter period of time. Compared to longhand, a typed report is neater and makes a better impression. When it comes to applying for a job, a typed resume is more professional. Another decided advantage of typing over writing is that typing is less tiring. Without any doubt, learning how to type can be a great asset.

The argument that typing is superior to writing is supported by four convincing reasons: getting a lot more done, neatness, looking professional, resulting in less fatigue. The presentation of these reasons makes the statement more than just an opinion. The non-typist who reads this paragraph may actually be inspired to learn this skill.

Follow-Up Exercise

What sort of specific information would you use for the following general statements?

1. The United States government should stop aiding foreign countries.

2. The microwave oven is far more effective than the gas type.

3. Everyone has had, sometime in his or her life, a frightening moment.

4. My cat Felix is the most adorable creature in the whole world.

5. Marriage laws should be made stricter.

PROBLEM

How can I be more specific in my writing?

A teacher comments: "You make some interesting points but they are too general. Be more specific."

Is this your problem when you write? If it is, you are in good company, for many people are too vague when they communicate in writing. More than speaking, effective writing demands very clear, concrete examples of any ideas you use.

Example 1: There are many things I do after school.

    Correction: There are many things I do after school, such as shop, clean the house, and do my homework.

Example 2: Jerry is a nice guy.

    Correction: Because he comes to my help when I need him, Jerry is a nice person.

Example 3: Earthquake is the greatest movie.

    Correction: The movie *Earthquake* is one of the best movies I ever saw because the catastrophe was so real and the acting so convincing.

Example 4: There are a lot of things I like.

    Correction: There are a lot of activities I enjoy, such as hiking, skiing, and collecting stamps.

Example 5: I feel lousy today.

    Correction: I feel sad today because I failed the geometry test.

Certain words in our language are very ambiguous (vague) and therefore should be avoided. In the examples above, you can see that "things," "nice," "greatest," and "lousy" do not convey any specific meaning.

The Crucible, by Arthur Miller, presents a view of a society that gets so fearsome that friends and neighbors are accused of witchcraft. Innocent people are brought to trial because of the paranoia that sets in. The author wants us to focus on what happens to a society when hysteria replaces common sense.

This paragraph is poor because it lacks specific detail. The general statement regarding the effects of fear in a society is interesting, and probably true, but there is nothing to back it up. We don't know, for example, *why* this fear takes over, *which* people are accused, and what relevance the book has to our day. Solution: What is missing are the specific details of setting, characterization, and conflict situation.

The Crucible, by Arthur Miller, presents a view of Salem, Massachusetts, in the 1600s. It is a society that becomes so fearful, because of witch-hunting, that the citizens begin to accuse friends and neighbors of consorting with the devil. Innocent people, like Goody Nurse and even the respectable John Proctor, are brought to trial because of the paranoia that sets in. The author wants us to focus on what happens to a particular society when the hysteria of even the dignified Reverend Danforth replaces common sense and makes him blind to the deceptions of a few troublemakers. The parallel to the McCarthy era in our recent history, when Communism was the enemy, becomes clear in the play.

In writing about literature, you must always include, as specific support, names of characters, relevant situations, the setting of the story, its meaning, and the focus of the story with regard to a problem or conflict.

Then we paddled down the river. We all took our places and were very scared. The water was rough. There were other dangers too. We never knew for certain whether we would make it back to shore. We kept looking at each other but we didn't talk. All we did was pray and hope for the best.

Solution

Use of a specific place, a sequence of events, and a description:

We all took bets we could paddle down the fierce river. Though we had no experience at it, we took our places — one at front, another in the middle, the third in the back — and, fearful and nervous, we thrust the canoe forward. The current was swift and the water beat roughly against the sides, tossing spray into our faces. It was too late to turn back and now we weren't sure whether we would make it back to shore. As our bodies moved like machines to avoid the logs in the water, we kept looking at each other for signs of confidence and assurance that everything would be all right. We were too busy rowing to talk. All we could manage, as the boat raced crazily down the water, was a prayer and a hope for the best.

PROBLEM

How can I make this descriptive passage more effective?

On a clear night you can see all the stars. They are so pretty at night. You look straight up and see everything bright and clear. It's like a dream come true to watch this show. You even feel good as you watch so many beautiful things happen right before your eyes.

Solution

On a clear night you can see a variety of stars and constellations. Planets, because of the reflected light, appear so still and pretty, and the stars, whirling in masses of burning gas, twinkle and seem to move so radiantly. You can look straight up with little difficulty and see everything — the North Star, the belt of Orion, and the Big Dipper — so bright and clear. All these millions of stars and the occasional meteors that shoot across the sky are like a cast of actors huddled thickly on a stage. It is a glorious show that can't be matched anywhere. As you watch such beauty unfold before you, you tend to feel inspired and awed by the spectacle of nature right before your appreciative eyes.

PROBLEM

How can I make this expository paragraph more effective?

Note how this writer attempts to explain a procedure but fails to make us understand it because of the lack of specifics.

The very first thing you have to learn if you want to go horseback riding is not to be scared. You have to mount the horse and make him know you are in control. Otherwise you may be in trouble, and bad things may happen. It's all a matter of making up your mind to be boss and master the situation. If you can do this, the animal will obey your commands.

Solution

The very first thing you have to learn if you want to go horseback riding is not to be scared because fear is self-defeating. Animals sense terror in humans and will get frightened themselves. Therefore, you have to practice mounting high objects a number of times and get accustomed to heights before you climb into the saddle of a horse. Otherwise, the horse may rear suddenly and throw you to the ground or it may simply gallop ahead. Holding the reins firmly, digging your toes into the stirrups, and keeping your body erect are ways of overcoming this problem. Psychologically, it is a challenge to master the situation and assert yourself over the horse. When you sit this way and utter calm but firm words to the horse, it will obey your commands.

PROBLEM

How can I make this argument more effective?

Note how this writer advances a point of view but fails to support it satisfactorily.

Quitting school is everybody's right. The principal can't make a student remain for a lot of reasons. Some kids are fed up with education and want to do something else with their lives. Why can't they be given this chance?

Solution

Quitting school to work is a right that should be granted young people at an earlier age than sixteen. It makes sense when you think about the numbers of students who have a poor record in school, who are truant, who misbehave in classes, or who are so turned off from school they don't even try at all. Forcing them to continue only adds a big burden to the school and the taxpayer. It would make more sense, for their own development as individuals, to allow such students to leave school at the age of fourteen so they can enter a trade and spend their time learning it.

Summary

Whether you are writing a description, a narration, an exposition, or an argumentation, the principle is the same: you must avoid generalities. The best way to overcome ambiguous language is to remember to explain key words you use. For example, in the paragraph above, the words "right," "reasons," "fed up," "something else," and "chance" need pinning down.

Our language lends itself to broad generalities but it is rich enough to give you the tools of crystal-clear expression. Part of good writing, then, is the search for richly specific and concrete language.

Follow-Up Exercise

Take any one of these ambiguous statements and develop it into a clearly defined paragraph. Use specific examples.

1. America is a wonderful country.

2. Lenny Bruce was an outrageous comedian.

3. Television is a waste of time.

4. Traveling is fun.

> **PROBLEM**
>
> How can I make my sentences more interesting?

1. The world is so full of pain and suffering. There are so many problems. I want to do something about it.

2. I went to Europe last summer. It was interesting. I had fun too. I went with my family. We traveled a lot. I saw many famous places.

What is wrong with these sentences? How can you improve them to make the writing more interesting?

> **PROBLEM**
>
> Your teacher reads a paper you have written and comments that your sentences are flat and dull. You are instructed to rewrite your paper, adding more interest and variety.

How do you do this?

Solution

Sentences can always be improved by doing one of the following:

1. Relating one sentence to another

2. Connecting sentences with transitional words

3. Modifying verbs with adverbs

4. Placing adjectives next to nouns

5. Adding dependent clauses

6. Lengthening or shortening a thought

Example

Here is a paragraph a student wrote. The teacher judged the sentences as uninteresting. Can you see why?

Every day at six o'clock sharp my family and I sit down to eat. My mother cooks the meals. My father helps set the table. We kids straighten up after. We sit down to eat together. We talk about the day's events. My father tells about his experiences on the job. My sister and I tell about what we did in school. Mother serves the food and then sits down to talk. My dog Lester jumps on our knees for food handouts. I feed him once in awhile. My father gets angry with me every time. My mother tries to make peace. Eating with my family can be fun. It is painful too.

Evaluation: The writing, although it does center around the family dinner, is flat and uninspiring because the sentences are:

1. Short and choppy

2. Unimaginative

3. Lacking in descriptive power

4. Unconnected and therefore not smooth

5. Do not reveal why the people act the way they do

Reconstruction: Now note the improvement in the same situation when the sentences are changed to (1) have variety, (2) include some description, (3) bear some relationship to one another, (4) reveal how and why people behave, and (5) have some complexity:

Every day at six o'clock sharp my family and I sit down *hungrily* to eat. My mother, *who loves cooking*, prepares the meals, *while* my father helps set the table *and* we kids *willingly* straighten up after. *Though we may be in different parts of the house*, we sit down together, *which is traditional in the family*. *During the course of the meal*, we talk *openly* about the day's events. My father, *who is an executive in an advertising agency*, tells about the experiences on the job. *When he is finished*, my sister and I tell about what we did in school. *At first*, Mother serves the food, *then* she sits down to talk. My dog Lester, *always grubbing for food*, jumps on our knees for handouts. *Since I take pity on him*, I feed him once in awhile. My father, *who believes in training a dog*, gets angry with me every time, *but* my mother, *who doesn't like fussing at the table*, tries to make peace. Eating with my family can be fun, *though I must admit it is painful at times*.

Evaluation: This depiction of the same situation, a family sitting down to eat together, contains sentences that are (1) of varying length, (2) imaginative, (3) descriptive, (4) connected and therefore unified, (5) more revealing of the family members. In short, because of the improved sentences, the whole account is far more alive and interesting.

Further Clarifications

1. If your sentences are *short and choppy*, think of ways of connecting them.

    Example: I hate school. It's so boring.

    Correction: I hate school because it's so boring.

2. If your sentences tend to be unimaginative, think of ways of lengthening them.

    Example: The summer is a great time. It's a time to have fun. I find it's also a time to relax.

    Correction: The summer is a perfect time to have fun and also an ideal opportunity to relax, like lying on the beach to get a beautiful tan.

3. If your sentences lack descriptive power, then look for ways to add adjective clauses.

    Example: My English teacher is the neatest dresser I have ever seen. His clothes really turn me on.

    Correction: My English teacher, who is very conscious about his appearance, is the neatest dresser I have ever seen. His clothes, which always show the latest fashion, really turn me on. Smartly attired, this man, young and handsome, wears clothes like a glove.

4. If your sentences do not follow smoothly, then you should look for ways of connecting them so that they have a relationship.

    Example: I just hate violent movies. They make me nauseous. I never go to see any.

    Correction: I hate violent movies *because* they nauseate me. *Therefore* I never go to see any.

5. If your sentences do not reveal how or why people act a certain way, then you should try to include adverbs.

    Example: Every time I come home late, my father gets up from bed to greet me. As I enter the house, he comes downstairs and talks with me.

    Correction: Every time I come home late, my father gets up *noisily* from bed to greet me *angrily*. Even when I enter the house *quietly so as not to be noticed*, he comes downstairs *hastily* and talks *endlessly* with me.

More Techniques

Still other techniques require a knowledge of grammar and syntax. But knowing them and knowing how to use them will certainly improve your sentences and make them more readable.

> Jerry watched television all night.
>
> Improvement 1 (appositive): Jerry, *a lazy person*, watched television all night.
>
> Improvement 2 (clause): *Since he didn't feel like doing his homework*, Jerry watched television all night.
>
> Improvement 3 (phrase): *In his room away from his family*, Jerry watched television all night.
>
> Improvement 4 (participle): *Lying on the bed in his room*, Jerry watched television all night.
>
> Improvement 5 (adjective): *Happy all by himself*, Jerry watched television all night.

These five changes are a good example of what you can do to enrich your sentences to give them more life. Try to do the same with this simple, unlively sentence:

My dog slept on the kitchen floor all day.

Follow-Up Exercises

Now look at the following paragraph to see whether you can point out all the ways this writer has managed to vary his sentences:

> A presidential election, a very important event, requires that all voters go to the polls. In doing so, voters are exercising their privilege to accept or reject candidates who may or may not be ideal for the top post of this country, one which calls for leadership and responsibility. If the citizens of this great country accept this need to speak out on election day, maybe better quality will result. Relying on the good sense of its electorate, this government operates in a democratic manner of wise expectation. Content with good results, each and every American can look to the process as beneficial to the nation. Therefore, because all men and women of age are duty-bound, we should turn out at the polls despite the poor choices for the office.

Now keeping in mind all the suggested techniques of good sentence structure, improve the following sentence units:

1. Jerry is my friend. He is always kind.

2. Vanilla is a delicious flavor.

3. School is boring. It is the same every day.

4. My brother is nice. My sister isn't.

5. I get up early in the morning.

HOW DO I SHOW CAUSE AND EFFECT?

(Credit: Leo de Wys, Inc.)

What *caused* this crowd to react this way?
What *effect* does this action have? On the teams? On the fans? On the community?

PROBLEM

How do I show cause and effect in writing?

Just about every situation in life has a cause and an effect. You may think of the cause as the action and the effect as the reaction. For example, if we catch a cold (the cause), we become weak and tired (effect). The virus that causes the coughing or sneezing is the action, while our weakened state is the reaction. Another example: a person smokes in bed and falls asleep with a lighted cigarette (the cause or the action), and therefore the house burns down (the effect or the reaction).

Here are some common illustrations of cause and effect relationships:

Cause	*Effect*
1. An actor is sensational in his role.	He receives many offers and becomes a star.
2. Factory workers are underpaid.	They go on strike.
3. A government is tyrannical and denies human rights.	The people rebel and overthrow that government.
4. A student is unmotivated in school.	He fails all his subjects.
5. Young people watch a lot of television.	They read few books.

You can show the relationship between cause and effect in a number of ways. Note how the action and reaction are brought together in the following sentences:

1. *Because* he was so sensational in his role, he received many offers and became a star.

2. The factory workers were *so* underpaid *that* they went on strike.

3. The people rebelled and took over, *for* the government was tyrannical and denied human rights.

4. *Because* he was unmotivated in school, Mario failed all his subjects.

5. *Because* young people watch a lot of television, they miss the opportunity to read many books.

Citing a Number of Causes for an Action

Sometimes there may be several causes (reasons) for a particular action or decision. Note how the following passage states one effect (reaction) which has many causes (actions).

EXAMPLE 1:

A typically hot summer day makes me very *lazy*. There's something about that sun beating down that *muddies* the brain and *relaxes* the muscles. When I lie on the beach gazing out on the calm ocean, I feel a sense of inertia that resists any kind of activity. Also, the sand underneath my body *cushions* me like a *soft* bed, and all I want to do is *dream* about exotic places. No question, when the temperature soars to ninety degrees in July, that's the time to cease movement and *stretch out* and let the hours *fly by*.

EXAMPLE 2:

Note how the causes of a disaster are given first and the effect stated last.

> Some say it was the river of lava that did it, while others claim it was the earthquake that ripped the ground and buried the city. Hot engulfing flames must have burned the buildings and suffocated all living creatures, and smoke no doubt cloaked the landscape in unprecedented horror. Whichever it was, the thriving roman city of Pompeii, long a citadel of pleasure and luxury, vanished forever from the face of the earth. *It was as if a page from the book of history were lost forever*.

Many causes are offered to explain the loss of the city of Pompeii. The last line states the reaction of the writer.

ASSIGNMENT

Write about some situation that has resulted from a number of causes. For example, how does the choice of a subject affect your work?

How do you do this?

STEP 1: THINK OF POSSIBILITIES

Think of a number of possibilities that show how one action results in another, how one decision brings about a certain result, or how one behavior affects another person. You might want to research the causes of slavery to see what changes it brought about; or you might want to investigate why there is so much crime in this country and deal with the effects on people; or you might decide to be personal and relate how your work or attitude has changed in a certain class.

STEP 2: OUTLINE THE FINAL EFFECT AND ITS CAUSES

Effect: I became a better student in my English class.

Cause 1: I was concerned about my poor grades in the first English class.

Cause 2: I came to a realization that I am responsible for everything I do.

Cause 3: I was fearful that, if I failed, I would not be accepted to college.

STEP 3: FLESH OUT EACH CAUSE WITH SPECIFIC ILLUSTRATIONS

In other words give more information about the causes of improvement in the new English class.

Cause 1: I was concerned about my poor grades in the first English class *because I had always been a good student. The results on tests, the criticisms of my compositions, and the warnings by my teacher at last made me wake up to a serious problem.*

Cause 2: I realized that I am responsible for everything I do. *Before, in my other class, it was easy to blame the teacher as mean and unfair and to think of the class as boring. But even if a teacher is not exactly the most exciting kind of person, or if the books I read do not turn me on, I still have a duty to myself to work and learn.*

Cause 3: I was afraid that, if I failed, I would not be accepted to college. *My future was involved directly with my efforts in school, and if I continued to goof off and blame others for my lack of success, I would not be accepted by the school of my choice. It was time to take myself in tow.*

STEP 4: THE CONCLUSION

What is the final statement you wish to make? What sort of emphasis will you place at the end to round out your writing?

STEP 5: FINAL ARRANGEMENT

The outline serves as the skeleton of the final job. Putting it all together involves what you have in the outline plus added examples and clarifications. Remember the purpose of this writing: to show a relationship between an effect and the causes that brought it about.

Becoming More Aware

Since I was changed from one English class to another, my work and attitude have improved. I owe this to a series of incidents and a maturity on my part. But becoming more aware was not an easy task.

I was concerned about my poor grades in the first English class because I had always been a good student. The results on tests, the criticisms of my compositions, and the warnings by my teacher at last made me wake up to a serious problem.

Luckily, I realized that I am responsible for everything I do. Before, in my other class, it was easy for me to blame the teacher as mean and unfair and to think of the class as boring. But even if a teacher is boring, or not exciting, or if the books I read do not turn me on, I still have a duty to myself to work and learn. It sounds so simple now.

To be honest, I was afraid that, if I failed, I would not be accepted to college. My future was involved directly with my efforts in school, and if I continued to goof off and blame others for my lack of success, I would not be accepted by the school of my choice. It was time to take myself in tow.

I am now much more honest about myself, and see that others are not to be held responsible for my attitude or manner. Realistically, I am the master of my own fate in school.

This student has adopted a healthier attitude (the effect) because of a series of incidents in school (the causes). We can say his desire to assume responsibility for himself has come about because of poor grades, a change of his English class, and certain realizations about school in general.

Follow-Up Exercise

Now write a short piece on some situation that shows cause and effect. You may select one of the following:

1. Television and violence

2. Sports and the fans

3. Discipline and behavior

4. School and learning

5. Drugs and values

HOW DO I BUILD TO A CLIMAX?

(Credit: Barton Silverman. From Leo de Wys, Inc.)

What will be the climax of this scene?

ASSIGNMENT

Write a paragraph dealing with a situation that builds to a dramatic ending.

How do you do this?

Naturally, if you tell the end of a story at the beginning, you may lose your audience. The trick is to get your readers to *want* to find out what happens at the end. You can do this if you know how to build one idea upon another, slowly but surely, until the excitement builds. The *climax*, then, is action resulting from the ideas you have built. Sometimes, you can end with an unexpected action, called a *climactic* close, but this action must be clearly believable from your build-up.

EXAMPLE 1:

When he first entered prison he was sad, but soon his depression grew, and he found himself alone, apart from other prisoners, deep within himself. Later, he lost his power to sleep, and he spent many nights walking the small space of his cell, talking aloud to himself. Even food held no attraction for him, and at times he didn't even bother to report to the dining hall. When others tried to converse with him, he looked away, and soon he barely heard anyone. An attempt to stimulate him with drugs, in the prison hospital, was useless; he just lay there, motionless. *Two years, three months, and two days after his imprisonment, the guard found him, kneeling over his cot, the blood gushing from a wound in his wrist. His depression was at last gone.*

Does the ending come as a surprise? Do all prisoners who are depressed commit suicide? Yet notice how the writer begins with the sadness of the inmate, how this turns to depression, and then finally the man's complete withdrawal. The last act, suicide, is one of a desperate man. The effect of the last two sentences is very dramatic and leaves the reader stunned. Yet the action was not unbelievable.

EXAMPLE 2:

Tragedy came in great leaps and bounds to the Jones family. First, the grandfather had a heart attack and died suddenly. No sooner did that happen than Jim Jones, the father, lost his job and could not find employment. Later, when Mary Jones, the mother, took ill with pneumonia, the house was in a turmoil. For Frank, the son, it was a trying time, made worse by his failure in school because of his need to work to support the family. After his sister Sue was involved in a serious auto accident, Frank became the one who assumed total responsibility for the house and the family. *What terrible thing would befall the Jones family next*?

Note how a series of terrible events strikes one family — the death of a grandfather, the father's loss of his job, the illness of the mother, and the sister's accident. All these events lead to a very real question, which the final sentence raises. It is the kind of question that makes the reader wonder why some people are so unlucky.

EXAMPLE 3:

He stepped forth upon the ridge to look up. The mountain top was still some miles off, hidden by low clouds. The path toward it was covered by snow. The wind ripped through his flesh with intensity. It was getting dark suddenly. The climber examined his bag to note how much food and how many matches were left. The decision had to be made now: continue or go back. *With a quick breath and a tensing of muscle, he placed his gloved hand on the next notch and moved forward.*

This is a tense situation, a physical challenge that we can all relate to. Before we get to the last sentence, we are unsure whether this climber will give up or not. The climax makes us aware of his courage in the face of danger.

EXAMPLE 4:

Sometimes the climactic statement can be made first and the background given after.

At last he became a full-grown man, ready to enter the world of adults. For too long, he had been pampered by his mother. His father, instead of directing his son to help around the house, did the jobs himself. Because of his charming manner, his teachers overlooked the boy's laziness and poor performance. Even his friends made decisions for him. But now, since his success in the intramural competition, he found the confidence and ego he had never had before.

This striking declaration that he was at last a man is contrasted with his life of indecision, laziness, and indifference. Mention of his success in sports accounts for a new image of himself that will help him to handle responsibilities better.

Follow-Up Exercise

Think of a situation or experience which led to a dramatic ending or climax. Write it in such a way that the details you use lead up to some unpredictable conclusion. You might write about:

1. A family problem

2. A school problem

3. A past incident

4. A meeting with friends

5. A party or celebration

HOW DO I ACHIEVE UNITY IN MY WRITING?

(Credit: Wide World Photos.)

Study this picture.
What do you see?

ASSIGNMENT

What are the unifying elements in this picture?

This picture has unity in the sense that the component parts that make up the whole scene are arranged in a specific way, each part related to the others.

How do you identify them?

Each person is positioned in such a way as to blend in with the others to create harmony and balance. If you removed any one detail, the picture would be less complete.

Analogy to writing: When you write a full-length essay or composition, you are arranging a series of paragraphs in a certain order to create an overall effect. That overall effect depends entirely on what point of view you choose and how you arrange the supporting details in relation to each other.

Unity, then, is a logical pattern of ideas in writing. If you glance back at that photograph, you can see the details as paragraph units creating the unity of a peaceful environment. The windows, for example, are the main focus of the scene because of the light they shed on the furniture. Actually, both windows *uniformly* serve the purpose of radiating light. Without them, the picture would be less effective.

When a paragraph unit is composed of sentences that effectively work toward an overall effect, it is considered *uniform*.

Unity in writing, it can be seen, leans heavily on uniformity of paragraphs.

EXAMPLE 1: UNITY IN DESCRIPTIVE WRITING

Note the details in the following paragraph and how they unite to build effect:

> New York City has a perennial charm that draws people to explore it. The theater district, with all its glitter, is a fantasyland that builds illusion out of reality. For variety and uniqueness, Greenwich Village has an endless stream of creative energy and an antiestablishment look that makes it a place to be relaxed in. And who can deny the splendor of ambling down Fifth Avenue and browsing in numerous shops that display fashion and elegance? Yes, New York City has the kind of attraction that makes other cities seem second-rate.

The opening or topic sentence conveys the basic idea, that New York is a charming city. The three supporting details — the theater district, Greenwich Village, and Fifth Avenue — are specific examples of charm. Together, the topic sentence and these three elements create an effect of unity.

EXAMPLE 2: UNITY IN NARRATION

Note how details in this narrative paragraph uniformly deal with an overriding idea.

> The body lay dry and useless on the shore. The waves of the ocean no longer lapped it indifferently. Scores of policemen and photographers hovered over the body as if attending a special guest. Even the doctor was bent in silent examination as he traced the man's eyes with a tiny light, illuminating them as if they were sapphires. A chorus of sea gulls added a

rhythm to the human movement around the dry, lifeless form. It was like a scene on a stage with the actors busily at work rehearsing parts.

The corpse and its effect on people and creatures is captured well in this paragraph. All of the details — the policemen, the doctor, and the sea gulls — join together in a unified image centered around the body. Thus, the stillness of death is contrasted with the activities of life.

EXAMPLE 3: UNITY IN ARGUMENTATION

Note how the position of the writer is uniformly strengthened by the supporting ideas:

The space program is an obvious waste of money that could benefit poor people. Instead of searching the craters of the moon, we could use that money in our neglected neighborhoods to build houses and recreation centers. Why bother trying to contact possible alien civilizations when the only civilization we are sure of is in need of food, shelter, and employment. In place of the sophisticated space centers at Houston and Cape Canaveral, we could easily have centers of new business where large numbers of our citizens could be trained for skills and technical jobs. To think that our government spends such a vast sum of our national budget on a program that seeks the unknown when the known needs on this earth are so evident is criminal!

EXAMPLE 4: UNITY IN EXPOSITION

Note how the procedure the writer is explaining is uniformly supported by the steps he thinks are important:

Mowing a lawn requires sense as well as skill. Even the most expensive mower must be used properly, with an eye to the weather and the condition of the grass. In wet weather it is best to leave the grass alone and wait for dry conditions; otherwise you will dull the blade of the machine and clog the draft system. Tall growth requires a setting that allows room for fast ejection of the clippings. Grass on rocky and sandy ground is best cut on a high setting so that the blade will not be chipped or the motor damaged. To preserve a machine and to cut a lawn successfully, you must know your mower as well as the basics of grass care.

Follow-Up Exercise

Think of an issue you wish to defend, or a procedure you would want to teach someone, or a scene that you could describe. State the idea or the effect and then support it with *three* reasons or details that unite to support the idea or effect.

Chapter Six

PREPARING FOR WRITING COMPETENCY TESTS

Why? Because some school districts may refuse diplomas to students who are not able to prove competence in writing. Many School Boards are now planning to test all secondary school students with a special examination, and unlike some short-answer tests you may have taken, these new writing tests will require you to prepare actual writing samples in several different forms.

PROBLEM

What is the test like?

Solution

The competency test usually consists of three types of writing tasks.

First, you will be required to write a business letter registering a complaint, asking for information, or ordering a product. Some possible topics for the business letter may involve situations such as:
1. Failure to receive a phonograph record ordered by mail
2. Refusal of a store to refund money for a defective toaster
3. Request for information about a product
4. Ordering an advertised product by mail

Second, you will be required to write a 150- to 200-word statement that will persuade the reader to your way of thinking. Some possible topics for this section of the examination might include writing a composition to:
1. The Board of Education recommending that a subject be added to the curriculum
2. The president of the local automobile association asking that organization to sponsor a Drive-a-Rama
3. The principal of your school requesting a fast food (similar to McDonald's) lunch program in your school

Third, you will be required to write a report based on facts and figures supplied in the test itself. For instance, you may have to write a report on:
1. A sporting event
2. An interview with a faculty member
3. A topic (the Mayan Indians) for social studies

PROBLEM

Who will evaluate your writing test?

Solution

Your English teacher will probably not mark your test, even though he or she will be involved in the grading process. Most competency tests will be read by more than one person, with each reader grading one part of the three-part test. That system will help you because if you have trouble with one part of the examination, the other readers won't be prejudiced against you. If, for instance, you score a 55 on the report, a 75 on the letter, and an 85 on the composition, your grade will average more than 70. Therefore, you will pass because 65 is the passing grade.

The teacher reading your answers will not compare your writing to that of other students in your class. Each teacher will receive copies of model answers, and your answer will have to meet certain standards that are reflected in the model answers. You may be the best writer in your class, but if your answer is not nearly as accurate as the model, you may still be given a low grade.

Unlike compositions, letters, and reports you have written for school classes, the answers on the competency test will not be given a grade based on specific errors. The rater will get an overall impression from your answer and compare it with the model. If yours is as good as the model or better, you will pass; if your answer is significantly worse than the model, you will fail.

Finally, the teacher grading your examination answer will be concerned with content, organization, and technical English. As a result, you should organize your writing carefully, prepare an overall plan, develop paragraphs fully, move from paragraph to paragraph and from sentence to sentence smoothly. Also, you want to be certain that you have provided the information requested in the instructions. In addition, knowing that emphasis will be placed on the mechanics of writing, you should observe the rules of sentence structure, spelling, punctuation, capitalization, and usage.

PROBLEM

How do I write a business letter for a competency test?

Solution

Let's examine a sample question and some answers.

Business Letter

Read the advertisement below:

> Green jade or brown tiger's-eye stone sus-
> pended within gold-plated heart. Necklace com-

plete with 18″ 14K gold-plated chain. Free
catalog with purchase. Money-back guarantee.
Allow 2–3 weeks for delivery. $3.98 plus 50¢
postage & handling.

BOX O' ROX
P.O. Box 1261,
Treehaven, N.H. 04567

Write a business letter ordering ONE of these necklaces for yourself or a friend. When
you write your business letter, be sure to:

1. Plan what you will write.

2. Give the company *all* the information it will need to fill your order.

3. Use an acceptable business letter form.

4. Write complete sentences.

5. Check your spelling, punctuation, capitalization, and usage.

Here are two model answers for the business letter assignment. Both are
satisfactory. How much material in each letter is absolutely essential for a passing
grade? Notice how the writers of the letters correctly selected *one* stone offered in the
advertisement. Observe how direct, and especially in the second letter, how brief their
letters are. Both writers made certain that the amount of money being sent was
mentioned in the letter. These letters are easy to understand, well organized, and
without serious errors. Finally, an acceptable business letter form is used correctly.

Model Business Letter #1

3215 South Street
Albany, New York 12208
January 19, 1979

Box O'Rox
P.O. Box 1261
Treehaven, New Hampshire 04567

Gentlemen:

Please send me the gold-plated, heart-shaped necklace you advertised in
January's *Teen Magazine.* I would like the necklace with a green jade stone.
Enclosed is a money order for $4.48 to cover the cost of the necklace, plus
postage and handling.

In your ad you say to allow 2–3 weeks for delivery. Since I would like to
give this necklace to a friend for her birthday in two weeks, I hope you will
rush delivery. Please send it to the above address.

Yours truly,

Davis Charles

Model Business Letter #2

476 North Street
Syracuse, New York 13205
July 24, 1979

Box O'Rox
P.O. Box 1261
Treehaven, New Hampshire 04567

Gentlemen:

Please send me one brown tiger's-eye stone necklace complete with 14K gold-plated chain as shown in your recent advertisement.

I have enclosed a money order for $4.48 to cover the cost of the necklace, plus postage and handling. Please send the necklace to the above address.

Sincerely,

Manny Seligman

The following sample business letter would probably not receive a passing grade on a competency test. The writer spells simple, common words incorrectly. The acceptable letter form is not always followed. The writer's order will be impossible to fill because his choice of stone is not given. Sentences are incomplete; basic punctuation rules have been broken. (For more information see Chapter 1 on the Business Letter.)

130 Elm Ave.
New Delmar, N.Y. 12054

Box O'Rox
P.O. box 1261
Treehaven
N.H. 04567

Dear sir, I would like to order one of your necklaces. I would like the coller to be green jade tigers eye suspended with gold plated heart.

I will send a money order for 3.98 plus 50¢.

Thank you

Frank James

PROBLEM

How do I write a composition for a competency test?

Solution

Let's examine a sample question and some answers.

COMPOSITION

1. The principal of your school is deciding whether or not to have a fast-food lunch program (similar to McDonald's) started in your school. The principal wants the opinion of each student. Decide whether you prefer the fast-food program or whether you prefer the lunch program you have in your school now. Write a composition of at least 150 words explaining your choice to the principal. Keep in mind that the purpose of your composition is to persuade the principal to choose the lunch program you prefer. Give at least two reasons for your choice. Explain each reason.

2. Since the purpose of your composition is to persuade the principal to agree with you, be sure to:
   a. state your opinion clearly
   b. explain your reasons carefully
   c. follow the rules for paragraphing, sentence structure, spelling, punctuation, capitalization, and usage

Here are two model answers for the composition assignment, both of which are quite satisfactory. They each meet all the requirements of the assignment. Notice the paragraphing, the careful explanation of the writers' reasons for their choices, the clear expression of opinion, the almost errorless technical English.

Composition #1

I feel that our school should retain its present lunch program rather than adopt the fast-food approach. With our present program, we are offered an interesting variety of meals, each carefully planned to provide a balanced diet. This variety is important not only from a nutritional standpoint but also from an educational point of view.

A fast-food menu consists of a fixed number of dishes, principally hamburgers and french fries. Fruits and vegetables are noticeably absent, as are other traditional entrees such as roast beef, turkey, chicken, fish, and ham. Fast-food dishes are invariably grilled or deep-fried, which provides plenty of calories but few of the required nutrients. Although it's fun to have this fare from time to time, it can soon become monotonous.

And shouldn't the school lunch be a learning experience? For many students, lunch is the main meal of the day. Our present lunch program teaches by example the value of a balanced diet and the virtue of variety in meals. Our school would lose a real teaching opportunity if it succumbed to the fast-food fad.

Composition #2

I think a fast-food lunch program would be a better choice than our present school lunch program because it would be more like a treat than a treatment. Our present program provides a balanced meal according to someone in the government who knows about these things; however, they do not seem to know what kids like to eat.

Many of the pupils paying for the current program only eat what they like. The rest is wasted. They do not have a balanced meal and they pay more for what they eat than it is worth. Some kids cannot afford it at all, and some would rather bring something better from home.

The school has a lot of people and time involved in planning and preparing and serving the meals that most kids do not appreciate. And that costs money. Why not let the fast-food company have the headaches, make sure everything is hot, and supply the kind of food kids like to eat?

I do not know about the rest of the students, but give me a Big Mac, fries, and hot apple pie and I'll be happy — and full.

Now read the following sample writing for the same assignment and answer the questions that follow it:

Composition #3

Yes I think we should have a fast food lunch program. That way, more persons will be eating lunch rather then throwing them away. Fast foods arent all that bad for you, they are meat and vegetables for the most part. If we get a fast food program in our school I think more persons will eat their lunch and get better health and still enjoy it because they wont be throwing their lunch in the garbage. And also people wont starve the rest of the day because they had to throw away their food because it was terrible. So they will enjoy their food and get nutrition from the meat and vegetables. And people will be happier. After all, who doesnt complain about the lunch they have now? So if you have to complain eat hamburgers and french fries and see for yourself.

What problems in writing does this student have?
How has a lack of paragraphs made this composition less effective?
What strengths in the composition compensate for the weakness in organization?
Where does the writer include two reasons to persuade his reader?
Although this sample is probably on the borderline of passing, what additional errors would make it a certain failure?
How could careful rewriting help this student improve the composition?

PROBLEM

How do I write a report for the competency test?

Solution

Let's examine a sample question and some answers.

REPORT

1. Read all of this question before you start to write.
2. You have been asked to look up some information on the Mayan Indians of Central America and write a brief report for your social studies class. You took the notes included in the box below:

   > NOTES
   > Ruins of large cities of stone still remain
   > Mainly in Southern Mexico and Guatemala
   > Studied moon, planets, stars
   > Played a kind of ball game on stone courts
   > Corn, other crops raised for food
   > Kingdoms about 300 A.D. to 1300 A.D.
   > Had picture writing
   > Way of life gone before Columbus came to America

3. Arrange and develop these notes into a report.
4. In your report be sure to:
   a. include all the information that is in the notes
   b. arrange the information according to a plan
   c. write complete sentences
   d. follow the rules for sentence structure, spelling, punctuation, capitalization, and usage

Here are two model answers for the report question. Note how different they are in length, though both are satisfactory answers. Observe also that the first writer chose to organize the material into three paragraphs while the second developed the material in one paragraph. Both writers competently placed the notes in a logical order and used words like "also" to tie the notes together. Both stated the main idea of the writing early in the answer.

The model answers include all of the notes in the instructions; no notes have been left out. The students had been so instructed and followed instructions, an important part of this test.

Good answers, as you see, are without serious technical flaws.

Model Report #1

Long before Columbus made his journey of discovery, a most remarkable culture developed in Central America. It was the culture of the Mayan Indians, who lived primarily in what is now known as southern Mexico and Guatemala.

The Mayan kingdom existed for a thousand years between 300 A.D. and 1300 A.D. The ruins of large cities built of stone remain to this day as mute testimony to the advanced nature of this civilization. There is also evidence that the Mayan Indians had learned the secret of raising corn and other crops for food.

The advances of the Mayan Indians, however, were not limited to food and shelter. They had learned to record their thoughts through picture writing, and they studied the moon, the planets, and the stars. They even played a kind of ball game on stone courts. Clearly, the culture of the Mayan Indians reached a high level of development in an isolated corner of the world.

Model Report #2

The Mayan kingdoms flourished in southern Mexico and in Guatemala about 300 A.D. to 1300 A.D. The Mayans were cultured, as shown by their picture writing and their studies of the moon, planets, and stars. They also played a kind of ball game on stone courts. Their food consisted mainly of corn and other agricultural crops. Although their way of life was gone before Columbus came to America, ruins of their large cities of stone still remain.

When we examine the student sample that follows, we see how easy it can be to write an unsatisfactory answer. In this sample, the student failed to read the question carefully. The writer missed entirely the fact that the notes were taken about the Mayan Indians of Central America. Then, instead of arranging the information according to a plan, the writer tried to string the notes together just as they had been listed. The sentences are not clear and, while all the information is included, it is not always understandable. There are also serious errors in technical English.

Model Report #3

Ruins of large cities of stone still remains in Mexico and Guatemala who studied moon planets stars by playing a game on stone courts. The people play and grow corn crop raised for food. These kingdom were about 300 A.D. to 1300 A.D. People had picture writing way of life before Columbus came to America.

FINAL THOUGHTS

This book has been designed to show that writing is a process more than a skill. The entire book rests on the principle that good writing results from good thinking. The actual commitment of words on paper in completion of an assignment is the end-result of several important stages: (1) Thinking through a topic, (2) Organizing and arranging ideas, (3) Making a decision as to how these ideas will be presented, (4) Outlining the ideas logically, (5) Fleshing out the outline with details and examples, (6) Writing a first draft, and (8) Composing the final product.

The mechanics of language — syntax, grammar, usage, spelling and vocabulary — are the tools that help build writing clarity but are not the primary means of writing effectively. They should be dealt with functionally after papers are examined. Diagnostically, common errors should emanate directly from student writing as a basis for reinforcement and drill.

Grammar is grammar, and writing is writing. If grammar is to be taught, it should be realistic in terms of student writing. The key question is: How will knowing this particular skill help to improve written communication in general? In short, the teaching of basic skills should not be confused with the process of acquiring confidence in writing.

And that is what this book has been all about: to show if any writing assignment is approached with a clear understanding of the preparatory thinking stages effective self-expression will be generated.

504 Absolutely Essential Words

by Murray Bromberg, Julius Liebb, Arthur Traiger
160 pp., paper $4.25

A self-help method of vocabulary development in forty-two lessons. Teaches essential words that are known and used regularly by educated people. Each new word is defined and used in three sample sentences. The words are then used in a brief article followed by exercises which help fix the word as a permanent part of the user's vocabulary. Once words are learned, they are used throughout the book to insure total mastery of each word. A basic book for learning important words used in newspapers, television, magazines, and conversations. With imaginative illustrations that aid learning.

Teach Yourself English

by William L. Young
128 pp., paper $3.75

This is a book for anyone wishing to improve their basic English. Barron's offers help for those for whom English is a second language, as well as help for native-born Americans who wish to strengthen their language skills at home. A programmed workbook, *Teach Yourself English* includes explanations of the part of speech, sentence style, punctuation, spelling, and diction. Practical for classroom teaching, diagnostic testing, assignments based on individual instruction techniques. Adults find that they can work at their own pace, on their own time, to achieve an English proficiency outside of the classroom.

Grammar—In Plain English

by Harriet Diamond and Phyllis Dutwin
228 pp., paper $6.50

A unique approach to grammar by way of a functional approach rather than an authoritarian way. Includes practice exercises and cumulative reviews. An excellent volume for adults preparing for the GED and college and university remedial language usage clinics. Contents included cover the simple sentence, agreement in time and number, addition and correction use of descriptive words and phrases, correct use of pronouns, understanding correct sentence structure, punctuation and capitalization, style and clarity of expression, commonly misspelled words and hints and rules for correct spelling, homonyms and correct word usage. *Grammar—In Plain English* also includes practice exercises and cumulative reviews.

Word Mastery:
A Guide to the Understanding of Words

by Marjorie Drabkin; Murray Bromberg, Editor
224 pp., $4.95

A comprehensive approach to vocabulary development utilizing words in context and exercises that explore the varied meanings of words. Provides an effective way to learn the terms found on aptitude tests and qualifying examinations for college and graduate schools. Gives instruction in understanding unfamiliar words through context and language clues. Outlines sources of lexical information and describes how word meanings develop.

Barron's Basic Word List

Samuel C. Brownstein and Mitchel Weiner
256 pp., paper $2.75

A pocket-sized word book that will help you increase your vocabulary at your own pace, in your free time. This convenient, small volume includes words and their meanings as well as practice exercises with answers.

Card Guide To English Grammar, Punctuation, And Usage

by Vincent F. Hopper
paper $1.50

A quick reference card that is always at the student's fingertips. All the fundamentals of grammar, condensed, but in type large enough to read easily; on a durable varnished card, punched to fit any 3-ring binder. This card can be used with any grammar textbook. A study aid that the student cannot afford to miss.

Vocabulary Builder

(A SYSTEMATIC PLAN FOR BUILDING A VOCABULARY. TESTING PROGRESS, AND APPLYING KNOWLEDGE)

by Samuel C. Brownstein and Mitchel Weiner
160 pp., paper $3.50

A programmed method of improving your vocabulary. Designed for the student preparing for vocabulary tests included on a variety of college admissions, psychological, scholarship, or achievement examinations. This systematic plan includes 2500 word entries, including all the words likely to be tested on the various types of vocabulary tests now being given.

BARRON'S EDUCATIONAL SERIES, INC.
113 Crossways Park Drive, Woodbury, New York 11797

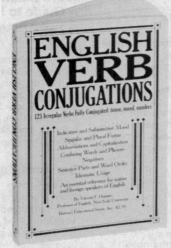

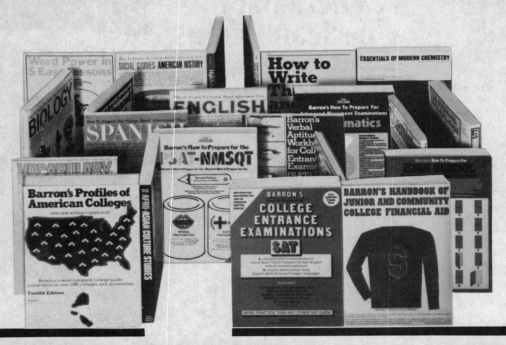

NOTES

NOTES